# JAMES JOYCE

# REFLECTIONS OF IRELAND

# JAMES JOYCE

# REFLECTIONS OF IRELAND

BERNARD McCABE · ALAIN LE GARSMEUR

LITTLE, BROWN AND COMPANY
BOSTON · TORONTO · LONDON

*For*

Dominic, Patrick and Rose

*and for*

Seamus and Marie

Photographs copyright © 1993 Alain Le Garsmeur
Introduction, Chronology and selection copyright © 1993 Bernard McCabe

First published in Great Britain in 1993 by
Little, Brown and Company (UK)
Brettenham House, Lancaster Place, London WC2E 7EN

The publishers wish to thank the Poetry/Rare Books Collection, State University of
New York at Buffalo for permission to reproduce the photograph in the Introduction.

ISBN 0-316-88893-1
A CIP catalogue record for this book
is available from the British Library

10 9 8 7 6 5 4 3 2

Designed by Bet Ayer
Typeset by SX Composing Ltd, Rayleigh, Essex
Printed and bound in Italy by Arnoldo Mondadori

Opposite title page: Mulligan's in Poolbeg Street

# CONTENTS

# A BRIEF CHRONOLOGY

**1882** James Aloysius Augustine Joyce born 2 February in Rathgar, a south Dublin suburb, to Mary Jane Murray and John Stanislaus Joyce, a comfortably-off middle class couple.
**1888** Enrolled as a boarder at the Jesuit Clongowes Wood College.
**1891** On top of other serious financial problems, John Joyce, a heavy drinker, loses his government job and the Joyces begin to shift their large family from one house to another to escape bailiffs. Joyce has to leave Clongowes.
**1893** Joyce briefly a pupil at a Christian Brothers' school, then given a scholarship at the Dublin Jesuit school, Belvedere.
**1894** Visits Cork with his father, who is selling up his last properties there.
**1894-8** Many academic successes at Belvedere. For a time very active in religious sodalities. But at about fourteen begins to seek out prostitutes in Dublin's red-light district.
**1898** Enters the Royal University (now University College Dublin). Concentrates on modern languages: French, Italian, German, and eventually Norwegian, in order to read Ibsen.
**1899** Refuses to sign student protest against Yeats's religious unorthodoxy in *The Countess Cathleen*.
**1900** 'Ibsen's New Drama' appears in the *Fortnightly Review*.
**1901** Attacks the Irish Literary Theatre in privately printed pamphlet, 'The Day of the Rabblement'. Refuses to take part in nationalist political and literary activities.
**1902** 'James Clarence Mangan' published in *St. Stephen's*, the college literary magazine. Meets Yeats, Lady Gregory and other Irish writers. Two book reviews in the English-owned Dublin *Daily Express*. Graduates. On 1 December goes to Paris to study medicine.
**1903** Twenty-one book reviews in the *Daily Express*. Meets Synge in Paris. In April returns to Dublin when told his mother is mortally ill. She dies in August.
**1904** Writes an essay-story, 'A Portrait of the Artist' (unpublished in Joyce's lifetime). Begins to rewrite it as *Stephen Hero* (also unpublished in his lifetime). Poems in various magazines. First *Dubliners* stories in *The Irish Homestead*. 'The Holy Office', a fierce verse attack on literary Dublin. Shares a concert platform with the great tenor, John McCormack. Shares the Sandycove Martello Tower with Oliver St. John Gogarty (the model for Buck Mulligan in *Ulysses*). Teaches for a time in a private boys' school in Dalkey. Meets Nora Barnacle, a Galway girl who is a chambermaid at Finn's Hotel in Dublin. They elope to Paris, Zurich, Trieste, then settle in Pola, where Joyce teaches in a Berlitz language school.
**1905** Move to Trieste. A son, Giorgio, born. Submits *Dubliners* (twelve of the eventual fifteen stories) to a Dublin publisher. Much financial and general assistance from his brother Stanislaus, through the next ten years.
**1906** Move to Rome. Works in a bank for minimal wages. Desperate money problems. Two more *Dubliners* stories written. He outlines then abandons a third, to be called 'Ulysses', the germ of the novel.
**1907** *Chamber Music*, his first small volume of poems, published in London. They move back to Trieste. Their daughter, Lucia, born. 'The Dead' completed. Begins work on *A Portrait of the*

Artist as a Young Man. Articles in *Il Piccolo della Sera*. The first of *Dubliners*' many rejections is announced.

**1908** First three chapters of *Portrait* completed. Has trouble going on with it.

**1909** Two trips to Ireland, without Nora. Signs contract for *Dubliners*. Helps to establish Dublin's first cinema, the Cinema Volta. In Trieste meets Italo Svevo, a model for Bloom.

**1910** The Volta fails. *Dubliners*' publication postponed.

**1911** Troubles with writing *Portrait* continue. He abandons it, and his sister Eileen rescues the manuscript from the fireplace.

**1912** Last trip to Dublin, with his family. Visits Galway and Dublin. Printers destroy sheets of *Dubliners*, calling the book obscene. 'Gas from a Burner', a scathing verse attack on publishers and printers.

**1913** Yeats offers help. Ezra Pound writes encouragingly.

**1914** *Portrait* published serially in *The Egoist* (London), the last chapter just meeting its deadline. *Dubliners* at last published. Begins writing his play, *Exiles*. Begins *Ulysses*.

**1915** To escape the First World War, moves to neutral Zurich. Finishes *Exiles*. Pension from Royal Literary Fund.

**1916** Civil List pension. *Portrait* published in New York.

**1917** First of Harriet Weaver's anonymous gifts of money arrives. Many more generous gifts from Miss Weaver will appear throughout his life. Eight poems in *Poetry* (Chicago). First eye operation.

**1918** *Little Review* (New York) starts serializing *Ulysses*. *Exiles* published in New York. Tentative, almost certainly never consummated, romantic affair with Marthe Fleischmann.

**1919** Back to Trieste. More teaching. One poem.

**1920** *Little Review* copies, containing *Ulysses* episodes, seized and destroyed as pornographic in New York. The Joyces move to Paris. Joyce can now at last abandon language teaching. Ezra Pound vigorously promotes his reputation. Serious rift with brother, Stanislaus.

**1922** *Ulysses* published in Paris by Shakespeare and Co. (Sylvia Beach and Adrienne Monnier.) Copies confiscated by British and American customs officers. Much acclaim in Europe and the USA.

**1923** Begins *Finnegans Wake*. T. S. Eliot publishes an influential review of *Ulysses*.

**1924** First fragment of the *Wake* published in the *transatlantic review* under the title 'Work in Progress'. Severe eye troubles again; they will continue for the rest of his life, with many operations.

**1925** More 'Work in Progress' published. Many negative responses from earlier admirers, among them H.G. Wells, Ezra Pound, Joyce's brother Stanislaus, and Harriet Weaver (who nevertheless continues her financial support).

**1926** *Ulysses* pirated in New York.

**1927** First of seventeen installments of 'Work in Progress' published in the literary review, *transition* (Paris). The last of these appears in 1937. *Ulysses* appears in German. His second and last book of poems, *Pomes Penyeach*, published in Paris, to a lukewarm reception.

**1929** French translation of *Ulysses* appears. Samuel Beckett begins to help Joyce with *Finnegans Wake* and Lucia develops a troubling attachment to him.

**1931** In July, Joyce and Nora marry in London. Joyce's father dies in December. Stuart Gilbert publishes his pioneering study of *Ulysses*, written with the author's detailed assistance.

**1932** His grandson, Stephen James Joyce, born in February. James writes his poem, 'Ecce Puer'. Lucia has a serious mental breakdown.

**1933** *Ulysses* judged not to be pornographic in New York courts.

**1934** *Ulysses* published in New York.

**1936** *Ulysses* published in London.

**1938** 'Work in Progress' completed. Its secret title, *Finnegans Wake*, revealed.

**1939** *Finnegans Wake* published in London and New York. Joyce disappointed at its unenthusiastic reception. War declared. Joyce much preoccupied with Lucia's health and treatment.

**1940** The Joyces forced to leave France. Back to Zurich; Lucia, too ill to join them, remains in a French hospital.

**1941** After months of anxiety and ill-health, Joyce dies of a perforated ulcer in Zurich. Nora survives him for ten years.

# LISTENING TO JOYCE

James Joyce, who found a hundred different styles to write in, found only one place to write about: the city of Dublin. In 1904, aged twenty-two, he had left that city for good, and apart from three fleeting visits a few years later, he never lived there again. But the thirty-seven years of self-exile in other men's cities – Trieste-Zurich-Paris – were passed in recalling, re-imagining and reworking successive versions of his home town. 'I always write about Dublin,' he told a friend, 'because if I can get to the heart of Dublin I can get to the heart of all the cities in the world.'

Joyce thought first that he was to be a poet, and occasionally through the years he would produce some delicate, pastoral lyric verses. But fiction was his true art. His first substantial publication, *Dubliners* (1914), is a collection of severe short stories about his fellow citizens. His first novel, *A Portrait of the Artist as a Young Man* (1916), brings to life the Dublin of Joyce's childhood, boyhood and youth in a troubled mixture of puzzlement, fascination and final rejection. His only play, *Exiles* (1918), dramatizes a fraught, anxious return to the city after long absence. In his last, extraordinary work, *Finnegans Wake* (1939), a vast all-night dream-sequence, written in dreamlanguage, he celebrates a Greater Dublin which, while remaining recognizably itself, is endlessly transformed into all the great cities of the world. Dublin's Hill of Howth becomes every mountain in the world; Dublin's River Liffey every river in the world; and Joyce's protagonists, a Dublin pub-keeper and his wife, by dream's magic, become that Hill and that River, and become archetypal Citizens of the World.

Before the *Wake* had come Joyce's masterpiece, *Ulysses* (1922). This epic, serio-comic novel offers, among much else, an anatomy of Dublin in 1904. Joyce built the framework of *Ulysses* with a down-to-earth attention to literal accuracies of time and place. 'I want,' he said, 'to give a picture of Dublin so complete that if the city suddenly disappeared from the earth it could be reconstructed out of my book.'

The city has not disappeared. Never mind this century's ugly destructions, and uglier constructions, cities like Dublin carry their history on their backs for all to see, just as their citizens echo that history in their talk, for all to hear. Joyce knew this. During those long years of exile his writing insistently presented a turn-of-the-century Dublin, in a sort of retrospective arrangement. And we, at the end of the century, can still look at Dublin in his terms.

Yet Dublin was not all of it; Joyce's memory and imagination did need to move outside the city's limits: over to Phoenix Park, out to the Hill of Howth – and sometimes beyond that, to the Clongowes Wood of his early childhood, into the not-so-distant Wicklow Hills, further away to his wife's native Galway, and down to Cork where his father had come from. So it is right that Alain Le Garsmeur's brilliant camera should follow him to those places, too. His photographs are not intended as 'illustrations' of Joyce's remarkable texts; the passage of time alone would make that seem incongruous. These pictures are offered rather as luminous revisitings of the places that Joyce made memorable. In *Ulysses* Joyce played, unobtrusively, with the word 'parallax', a technical

8

Nora and Joyce in Zurich

term for the way an object viewed from different points of vantage appears differently; and the novel exuberantly exploits this phenomenon. As Alain Le Garsmeur views Dublin and all Ireland modulated by Joyce's texts he similarly adopts his own varied points of vantage, and the reader will find the resultant visions of the city and the country to be as surprising as they are revealing.

Joyce's art typically transforms an intense perception of the ordinary into the extraordinary. His chosen word for such moments of vision was borrowed from the Catholic tradition that so deeply informed this Jesuit-educated lapser's heart and mind: epiphany. Epiphany means 'a showing forth', and Joyce delighted in showing forth the art that could be made out of what he had seen. *Reflections of Ireland*, then, with its juxtapositions of texts and pictures, is offered first as a celebration of Joyce's eye.

As such it speaks for itself. But Joyce's art is as much made out of what he heard as of what he saw. His original notebook collection of fifty epiphanies, which has survived and has been published, divides evenly into visual and aural perceptions. And when in *Finnegans Wake* Joyce carefully projects versions of himself into contrasting twin brothers, Shem and Shaun, the soberer Shaun the Post is a kind of cameraman, a recording eye, but his imaginative and more difficult brother, Shem the Penman, is 'all ears'. So this brief introductory survey of Joyce's life and work picks up that tip and lays a counterbalancing stress on the latter organ, offering a modest celebration of precisely that: Joyce's ear, with its marvellously exact chronicling of how people talk, and of how much can be said in talk. It is true that at certain moments in *Ulysses*, and through most of *Finnegans Wake*, Joyce downs the traditional novelist's tools of dialogue and narration, and takes off in a poet's self-delighting revelment, urgently exhilarating moments when language seems to become its own subject. And it is true that such word-play dazzles, overwhelms and moves us beyond casual notions of reality. Yet especially at such moments, the sustaining power beneath his work is the reality of a true vernacular, a true speaking voice. Joyce's creative happiness in the rhythms and inflections of the voice guarantees his humanity and makes his work exciting, beautiful, and, because it is the Dublin voice that he is dealing with, often very funny.

Joyce grew up in a depressed and oppressed Dublin that seemed, after the death of Parnell in 1891, to have lost its way. His own family's history echoes a general sense of collapse and decay. His father, John Joyce, model for the Simon Dedalus of his fiction, though clearly companionable, witty and quick-tongued, was also a dissolute and improvident man who, having squandered a considerable family inheritance, then drank his way out of a comfortable job in the city's administration.

9

So his large family, of which James was the eldest surviving child, shuffled dismally down through the various levels of Dublin housing and Dublin society. Joyce senior, in the manner of such men, seems to have known all or most of Dublin's drinking places, and most of Dublin's drinkers, especially the characters amongst them, and so, in time, did his son. When Joyce began writing his first book, in 1903-4, his ear was full of Dublin talk, Dublin voices.

The tone in *Dubliners* is studiously distant. Joyce was already affecting the stance of the artist he was to describe in *Portrait* as 'beyond or above his handiwork'. But the stories were evidently composed in the full flow of a young man's angry and bitter rejection of his background. The book presents his native city, he told an editor, in terms of 'paralysis' and with 'a special odour of corruption'. In *Dubliners* Joyce's cold eye rests on what is drab and squalid in the city and his cold ear catches the banality and emptiness of its citizens' talk. His characters are physically or morally paralyzed: Farrington, for example, in 'Counterparts', a drunk and a childbeater, or trapped Bob Doran, bullied into wedlock in 'The Boarding House', or the voyeurish Lenehan in 'Two Gallants', parasitical as well as paralyzed. Such figures were drawn, Joyce declared, in a phrase that has echoed down the years, 'in a style of scrupulous meanness'.

Meanness is certainly part of the innovative art of *Dubliners*, where Joyce remarkably manages to infect the narrative text with the sensibilities of his characters. But in the best stories his wonderful ear already supplies something richer: the serious and comic life in the human voices he records. To a prospective editor he spoke of his book, rather ominously, as 'a chapter in the moral history of my country'. But that distanced style prohibits any awkward judgmental intrusions. His Dubliners do condemn themselves out of their own mouths (think of Corley in 'Two Gallants'), but their live voices as often as not arouse human sympathy of a kind that can rescue for the reader even such lost figures as Lenehan and Farrington. Then *Dubliners* doesn't seem so scrupulously mean after all.

Take this brief exchange, offered without comment in 'Ivy Day in the Committee Room':

The old man . . . began to fan the fire slowly while his companion smoked.

– Ah, yes, he said, continuing, it's hard to know what way to bring up children. Now who'd think he'd turn out like that! I sent him to the Christian Brothers and I done what I could for him, and there he goes boosing about. I tried to make him someway decent.

He replaced the cardboard wearily.

– Only I'm an old man now I'd change his tune for him. I'd take the stick to his back and beat him while I could stand over him – as I done many a time before. The mother, you know, she cocks him up with this and that. . . .

– That's what ruins children, said Mr O'Connor.

– To be sure it is, said the old man. And little thanks you get for it, only impudence. He takes th'upper hand of me whenever he sees I've a sup taken. What's the world coming to when sons speaks that way to their father?

– What age is he? said Mr O'Connor.

– Nineteen, said the old man.

– Why don't you put him to something?

– Sure, amn't I never done at the drunken bowsy ever since he left school? *I won't keep you*, I says. *You must get a job for yourself*. But, sure, it's worse whenever he gets a job; he drinks it all.

Mr O'Connor shook his head in sympathy, and the old man fell silent, gazing into the fire.

The old man, comic and sad, reveals that he has made his son in his own image, repeating a pattern in *Dubliners* of citizens circling about themselves. The fatigued rhetoric about bringing up children heralds all the other false rhetorics in the story. Rhetoric celebrated as it betrays itself is a device found everywhere in Joyce. In 'Ivy Day' he proffers perhaps his meanest view of grey, sunken Dublin in the post-Parnell years. As a group of election canvassers meet and mutter together, mention of the dead king of Irish politics only emphasizes the emptiness of the occasion. They worry about getting paid:

– O, he's as tricky as they make 'em, said Mr Henchy. He hasn't got those little pigs' eyes for nothing. Blast his soul! Couldn't he pay up like a man instead of: *O, now Mr Henchy, I must speak to Mr Fanning. . . . I've spent a lot of money.* Mean little shoeboy of hell! I suppose he forgets the time his little old father kept the hand-me-down shop in Mary's Lane.

– But is that a fact? asked Mr O'Connor.

– God, yes, said Mr Henchy. Did you never hear that?

'Mean little shoeboy of hell!'. . . . 'Sure, amn't I never done at the drunken bowsy ever since he left school?' Meanness and moralizing scatter in the sad comic life of such voices. *Dubliners'* crowning and concluding story, 'The Dead', deploys them in marvellously varied abundance. 'The Dead', really a novella, shares all the innovative methods of the earlier tales: the deadpan stance, the sly ways in which narration slips without warning into the tones of its characters, into their variously limited worlds. Yet it is a different kind of story.

When the twenty-two-year-old Joyce left Dublin in 1904 he took with him Nora Barnacle, the valiant Galway woman who was to be his life-long companion, the mother of his son and daughter, and eventually (in 1931) his wife. By 1907, when he came to write 'The Dead' and added it on to his *Dubliners* collection, Joyce had spent three years scratching a living as a language teacher in Trieste (with a bleaker interlude as a bank clerk in Rome). He had lived three years of conjugal life, and he was now the father of a child. Trieste was a cosmopolitan city and Joyce had met many members of its bourgeoisie, but also writers, painters, bohemians. In short, by now he knew a lot more. And, at this safe distance, he was beginning to feel some real nostalgia. 'I've been unnecessarily harsh to Dublin,' he wrote in his lordly way to his brother Stanislaus. The cheerful Christmas celebrations in 'The Dead' suggest a move towards reconciliation. Dublin's trapped citizens are still there, but there's a maturer imaginative sympathy with them, and with what the city itself has to offer.

More importantly, the artist now literally takes on matters of life and death, dealing with them with a strangely disturbing power. Critical attention to 'The Dead' tends to concentrate on its striking conclusion, on the organ-swell of its last pages: the all-encompassing, all-reconciling vision of snow falling over Ireland, uniting the living and the dead. Yet the story's peculiar strength surely springs from the cornucopia of voices that creates its distinctive comic and troubled world: at the dancing, at dinner, on the stairs, out in the pantry, out in the snow, and, at last, in the dark bedroom.

Typical of 'The Dead''s sure-tongued accuracy are two of the several thrusts made at embattled Gabriel Conroy's soul in the course of this celebratory Christmas-time evening. First, as the story opens, comes Lily the caretaker's daughter, with her bitter response to Gabriel's bland gallantries: 'The men that is now is only all palaver and what they can get out of you.' Another comes near the end, as Joyce obliquely introduces the theme of actual or spiritual cuckoldry (a theme that was to haunt the rest of his work). Gabriel's wife, Gretta, speaks simply and devastatingly about the death of an earlier unsuspected lover:

– I implored of him to go home at once and told him he would get his death in the rain. But he said he did not want to live. . . . And when I was only a week in the convent he died and he was buried in Oughterard, where his people came from. O, the day I heard that, that he was dead!

She stopped, choking with sobs. . . .

Such precision in catching the contrasting tones, the flat yet rhythmic harshness of the Dublin girl, the gentle grief of the woman from Galway, show Joyce at twenty-five already master of the intense realism he was to deploy in such telling and devious ways throughout the rest of his life's work.

---

In 1904 Joyce began an autobiographical novel that he called *Stephen Hero*. Unhappy with the writing, he put it aside, having destroyed most of it. The surviving chapters were retrieved and published in the USA some years after Joyce's death. (How he would have hated that enterprise, seen it as an aesthetic betrayal.) But *Stephen Hero* is there now and once read it cannot be forgotten. It is fascinating in itself, and it modifies, even enlarges, our understanding of Joyce's aims in *A Portrait of the Artist as a Young Man.* Stephen Dedalus first appears here as twenty-year-old 'Daedalus', a difficult, prickly figure, intelligent, conceited, impatient, socially uneasy, sexually uneasy. *Stephen Hero* is written plain. Sometimes its fresh realism can be powerful and painful, but it has a lumpy everydayness about it that evidently displeased its author. He dropped it for three years, then set about rewriting it, obliquely, elusively, allusively, paring it down and reshaping Stephen Dedalus to suit the more profound and complex aims he had for this book.

*Portrait*'s five long chapters tell the story of a child, an adolescent, and a young man struggling to understand the Dublin world he is thrust into, and struggling to free himself from its bonds, the nets he must fly past. The road to freedom, Stephen Dedalus discovers, is through art; only through art can he order and re-create his world.

Joyce had already used various expressive structuring systems in *Dubliners*: patterns of language, thematic orderings. Such orderings thrust themselves at us in *Portrait*. Dedalus's strange name tells us that he is a representative, a symbolic figure as well as being the young man we come to know. The first pages sow thematic seeds of all kinds. They set a series of images and symbols aflutter – images of flight, water and colour – as a whole symbolic apparatus works to intensify the reader's hold on Stephen's world and develop the meaning of his physical, spiritual and aesthetic experiences.

And it's all very interesting. But most interesting, and most memorable, is the series of voices that Joyce uses to dramatize and embody Stephen's shifting understanding of what's happening to him. The first voice in *Portrait* speaks baby-talk, as Stephen's father tells him a puzzling nursery story:

> Once upon a time and a very good time it was there was a moocow coming down along the road and this moocow that was coming down along the road met a nicens little boy named baby tuckoo. . . .

Then subjugation begins: *Pull out his eyes,/Apologize.* And Stephen must endure many more oppressive and opprobrious voices before, at twenty-one, he finds his own hero-artist's voice, now in triumphant brag as he leaves Dublin for Paris: 'I go to encounter for the millionth time the reality of experience and to forge in the smithy of my soul the uncreated conscience of my race.'

*Portrait* offers some celebrated vocal set-pieces: Father Arnall's fearsome school-retreat sermons about Hell, Stephen's peripatetic disquisitions on aesthetics. Yet those formal discourses, convincingly recorded though they are, come less close to the bone than do moments when Joyce's ear is more quiveringly alert: Stephen as a frightened small boy at school facing adult injustice and a priest's hard leather on his shrinking flesh: 'The door opened quietly and closed . . . "Out here. Dedalus. Lazy little schemer. . . . Out with your hand this moment!"' Or Stephen at family Christmas dinner, puzzled, excited and frightened by adult argument and tears: by his aunt, Dante, stiff in the rhetoric of provincial piety, by his father and Mr Casey, whisky-laden, egging each other on to excesses of priest-baiting and half-maudlin yet moving Parnell-worship – the whole a brilliant short story in itself:

> – There could be neither luck nor grace, Dante said, in a house where there is no respect for the pastors of the church.
> Mr Dedalus threw his knife and fork noisily on his plate.
> – Respect! he said. Is it for Billy with the lip or for the tub of guts up in Armagh? Respect!
> – Princes of the church, said Mr Casey with slow scorn.
> – Lord Leitrim's coachman, yes, said Mr Dedalus.
> – They are the Lord's anointed, Dante said. They are an honour to their country.
> – Tub of guts, said Mr Dedalus coarsely. He has a handsome face, mind you, in repose. You should see that fellow lapping up his bacon and cabbage of a cold winter's day. O Johnny!
> He twisted his features into a grimace of heavy bestiality and made a lapping noise with his lips.
> – Really, Simon, said Mrs Dedalus, you should not speak that way before Stephen. It's not right.
> – O, he'll remember all this when he grows up, said Dante hotly – the language he heard against God and religion and priests in his own home.

And of course Joyce himself did remember the language, as he no doubt remembered a journey to Cork with his spendthrift father when he was twelve. He later transformed it into the picture in *Portrait* of the adolescent Stephen, confused and heavy-headed about his growing sexual desires and fantasies, envying his father's 'rude, male health' yet cringing at his bar-room jovialities:

> – Your father, said the little old man to Stephen, was the boldest flirt in the city of Cork in his day. Do you know that?
>
> Stephen looked down and studied the tiled floor of the bar into which they had drifted.
>
> – Now don't be putting ideas into his head, said Mr Dedalus. Leave him to his Maker.
>
> – Yerra, sure I wouldn't put any ideas into his head. I'm old enough to be his grandfather. . . .
>
> – We're as old as we feel, Johnny, said Mr Dedalus. And just finish what you have there, and we'll have another. Here, Tim or Tom or whatever your name is, give us the same again here. By God, I don't feel more than eighteen myself. There's that son of mine there not half my age and I'm a better man then he is any day of the week. . . .
>
> – But he'll beat you here, said the little old man, tapping his forehead and raising his glass to drain it.
>
> – Well, I hope he'll be as good a man as his father. That's all I can say, said Mr Dedalus.

Such a moment is a true Joycean epiphany: 'a sudden spiritual manifestation, whether in the vulgarity of speech or gesture, or in a memorable phrase of the mind itself,' as he puts it in *Stephen Hero*. Such vulgarity, in the true sense of that word, can be found in Stephen's half-stifled talks with two Jesuit priests, one of whom explores the possibility of a priestly vocation for him. Stephen rejects this not unflattering invitation in order to become, in a memorable phrase of the mind, 'a priest of eternal imagination, transmuting the daily bread of experience into the radiant body of everlasting life.'

And Joyce's ear finds memorably beautiful cadences in Stephen's 'peasant' friend Davin's tale of an encounter with a lonely young wife in the western hills (see page 66). This story of 'the hidden ways of Irish life' is enthralling for Stephen, but also very disturbing, with its luring darkly secret sexual burden and its message of male uncertainty about female sexuality. 'Bat-like' is Joyce's odd term – an image that strangely flutters up again in *Ulysses*. This episode is pivotal in *Portrait*'s examination of the contradictions·of mind and body. Davin's voice echoes on in the book, with its gentle rhythmic phrasing and resonant simplicity setting up a curious tension in Stephen's and the reader's mind.

Voices are managed with great subtlety in *Portrait*. For instance, that last ardent cry, 'I go to encounter. . . .' would be a hard line to read, with its troubling edge of adolescent naïveté, were we not carefully prepared for it. But by now Joyce has given us so many variations on what it is to be a young man and an aspiring artist that the touch of magniloquence seems in the end perfectly ordered and earned.

---

Joyce finished *Portrait* in 1914 and a first complete edition appeared in New York in 1916. *Ulysses* was first published in its entirety in 1922. By this time Joyce had become known worldwide. But behind these bald facts lies a turbulent history of struggle for survival.

Trieste was especially hard going. Joyce lived there literally from hand to mouth, cadging where he could, drudging when he had to as an ill-paid teacher of English. Like his father before him he was a spendthrift, living extravagantly on any money he could lay his hands on and, again like his father, spending a lot of time dodging creditors, shifting from flat to shabby flat. And all the time there was the depressing battle, not for recognition – word was beginning to spread about the remarkable gifts of this startling new writer – but for publication, as timid editors and printers quailed before his outspoken work.

It had taken at least ten years to get *Dubliners* into print. *Portrait*, though long in the writing, had less of a rough ride. But when *Ulysses* began appearing serially in New York's *Little Review* in 1918, outraged protests about blasphemy and obscenity ensured that in 1920 the US Post Office confiscated and burned the first four issues containing it. Finally, Joyce, desperate to see his book published somewhere, agreed to a Paris

13

edition (1922). Quickly banned in the USA and in Britain, it was only after years of litigation that the book could be printed in New York (1934) and in London (1936). *Ulysses* had become a sort of contraband, wrapped in guilty brown paper. Yet it was not hard to find in Dublin; P. S. Hegarty's Irish Bookshop in Dawson Street, for example, sold it freely, though sometimes from under the counter.

Joyce had begun *Ulysses* in Trieste, but by 1915 World War One drove him to neutral Zurich, where he spent four years working steadily on his new manuscript. Eventually, in 1920, he settled in Paris and lived and worked there for most of the rest of his life. In the early *Ulysses* days he also completed his one play, *Exiles*. This drama, with its painfully strained examination of the velleities of cuckoldom as a central theme, is inevitably important to any Joyce enthusiast. But it finds no place in this book, for *Exiles* offers little or nothing to the eye, and, in its formal, even stilted exchanges, Joyce for once seems largely to have turned his ear away from the life-giving, life-enhancing Dublin vernacular.

*Ulysses* is another matter entirely. Among its large cast many of the inhabitants of *Dubliners* reappear, most of them talking. And a host of new ones are added, often enough 'translations' from Trieste and Zurich. In fact, two of the three central figures in *Ulysses*, Leopold Bloom and his wife Molly, derive largely, naturally enough, from Joyce's encounters during his years of exile. The third figure is *Portrait*'s Stephen Dedalus. In simple terms, the novel is an account of a single day – 16 June 1904, now universally known as 'Bloomsday' – in the lives of these three characters.

Stephen is back from his Paris adventure, having achieved nothing at all in the smithy of his soul. His mother has died after a painful illness; he is estranged from his improvident father and he is living in an abandoned Martello tower with Buck Mulligan, a clever, overbearing medical student. In the course of his long, mostly melancholy day, Stephen loses his home to the usurper, Mulligan, abandons his job after a morning's desultory school-teaching, attempts, unsuccessfully, to impress a group of Dublin *literati* with some cleverly fantastical theories about *Hamlet* and Hamlet's lost father, and passes the rest of his time in idle talk and drinking among Dublin's loafers. He wanders without purpose about the city until, abandoned by his companions, he ends up very drunk in a brothel in 'Nighttown', as Joyce calls the old Dublin red-light district. Outside it he is knocked down by a drunken English soldier.

Leopold Bloom is a small-time Jewish advertizing canvasser, married to a gentile wife, Molly, by whom he has a fifteen-year-old daughter, Milly. Bloom, too, has reason for melancholy. The death of his father, a suicide, and of his infant son, linger always in his mind, as does the certain knowledge that his wife has an assignation that day with another usurper, 'Blazes' Boylan, an entrepreneur and man-about-town. This betrayal is made more poignant for Bloom because he has had no full sexual relations with Molly since his son, Rudy's, birth and untimely death over ten years before. But, unlike Stephen, Bloom moves purposefully about Dublin, going about his precarious business, attending a funeral, visiting a woman on the point of giving birth, doing other small, charitable deeds and, incidentally, pursuing small, furtive sexual excitements.

At the end of a day in which their paths have casually crossed without communication, Bloom catches sight of drunken Stephen, follows him and rescues him from his troubles with English soldiers. Bloom takes him home; they talk, mutedly, fatiguedly, and the two part, perhaps to meet again, perhaps not. Each has suffered a number of oppressions and slights during the day: Stephen, for example, as exploited friend, rejected son, ignored artist, and Bloom as frustrated small businessman, as suspected cuckold, as known Jew. Both have been made to feel outsiders; now they have met. Nothing dramatic happens, but really and symbolically, an artist has met a citizen, a son has met a father, a Greek has met a Jew.

Shapely, plump Molly Bloom, a singer with a repertoire of light-classical and popular concert-party songs (of the kind Joyce loved) spends most of her day in bed; at first by herself, then in the afternoon with Boylan, and late at night with her husband, the returned wanderer. In the long final episode of

*Ulysses*, Molly muses sleepily over herself, her daughter, her lost son, and various men: her real and fantasized past lovers, the recently departed and unsatisfactory Boylan, the intriguing young visitor, Stephen, but above all her husband, Leopold – 'Poldy' – to whom her mind turns back again and again as the book ends in her gently erotic reveries.

———

*Ulysses* has various obvious themes. On the daily plane, it is about husbands and wives, fathers and sons, fathers and daughters, and about the vagaries of sexuality that play about individual and family life. It is about birth and death, and, in Joyce's reticent way, it is about 'that word known to all men,': love. Dublin, 1904, is there as a modern metropolis, with its trams and trains, its markets and monuments, its grand public institutions, great homes and deplorable slums. Joyce shows us it all with meticulous, almost superstitious attention to topographical exactitude, and with historical exactitude. He does not forget, for instance, to evoke the strains – social, economic and political – that are imposed on a colonized city, with its Vice Regal Lodge, and William Humble, Earl of Dudley, in charge. But especially again and again he marshalls all the senses, sight, sound, taste, smell, to present the feel of the place and its people:

> Hot mockturtle vapour and steam of newbaked jampuffs rolypoly poured out from Harrison's. The heavy noonreek tickled the top of Mr Bloom's gullet.
>
> Swish and soft flop her stays made on the bed. Always warm from her. Always like to let herself out. Sitting there after till near two, taking out her hairpins.
>
> A squad of constables debouched from College street, marching in Indian file. Goose step. Food heated faces, sweating helmets, patting their truncheons. After their feed with a good load of fat soup under their belts. . . . Let out to graze.
>
> Same blue serge dress she had two years ago, the nap bleaching. Seen its best days. Wispish hair over her ears. And that dowdy toque, three old grapes to take the harm out of it.

*Ulysses* develops *Portrait*'s enquiry into the nature of art and of the artist's necessary encounter with life. Stephen meets Bloom. The novel's subject is also, in the modernist way, itself, and the way it is being written; it's about what can be done, what can be performed with words. The title offers Joyce's broadest hint; this is to be a serio-comic version of the ancient Homeric epic. Bloom is a modern Ulysses, an everyday hero in a modern city; Molly begins as the nymph Calypso and ends as a Penelope, faithful to Bloom, after her fashion; Stephen is a lost Telemachus searching for a spiritual father. Dozens of minor characters swelling the Dublin scene turn out to have matching identities in Homer. One example: an enraged, blinded, giant Cyclops, hurling a rock at the escaping Ulysses becomes a half-drunk Irish patriot, blinded with rage, hurling a biscuit-tin after Bloom as he escapes from an argument in Barney Kiernan's pub.

This episode, moreover, is a parallax chapter: it is narrated in gigantically alternating voices; one adopts for a while the overblown periods of Irish patriotic writing, the other drones out a sardonic, wonderfully hard-hearted Dublin drinker's tirade. The latter voice is especially memorable. Here it is re-telling Bob Doran's sad story from *Dubliners* in one searing paragraph:

> Then see him of a Sunday with his little concubine of a wife, and she wagging her tail up the aisle of the chapel, with her patent boots on her, no less, and her violets, nice as pie, doing the little lady. Jack Mooney's sister. And the old prostitute of a mother procuring rooms to street couples. Gob, Jack made him toe the line. Told him if he didn't patch up the pot, Jesus, he'd kick the shite out of him.

The ironies in 'Cyclops', as elsewhere, are obvious enough: there can be no heroes in a modern epic. But the Homeric references, like other patterning devices and performances, verbal tricks and echoes, displays of learning and parodies, are there to impose an expressive artists's order on to teeming daily life, on to disordered nature. The ingenuities in *Ulysses* are considerable. The musical 'Sirens' episode mimics the development of a fugue; another episode is spoken in a girls' magazine sugariness; a third is told entirely in clichés. 'Circe'

15

offers a kind of nightmare pantomime in which a thousand voices rising from their daytime encounters dramatize, for example, Stephen's morning guilts and fears about his mother's death and Bloom's masochistic ambiguities about Molly's afternoon adventure. In 'Oxen of the Sun', set in the Maternity Hospital, we must not only recognize a parodic history of the gestation of modern English prose, but a simultaneous imitation of the growth of the foetus in the womb.

Reading *Ulysses* can sometimes seem a daunting experience, but excessive deference is out of place. Throw an occasional knowing and respectful nod at a Homeric parallel or two by all means (most of them, one suspects, were more useful to the writer as an organizing matrix than they are to the reader), and raise a high-grade hat to the host of pleasing ingenuities. Note the innovative modernisms and admire Joyce's prophetic experiments in meta-fiction. But in the end, gratefully recognize that amidst all the labyrinthine artifice of the book, it is nature that wins the ultimate victory. The pleasurable paradox is that the ordered pages of *Ulysses* leave us with the experience of something marvellously life-like and disorderly, the natural disorder of Dublin talk.

The novel is crammed with voices. Their rich polyphony leaps out in the first episode, on that brilliantly realized bright June morning as Stephen and Buck Mulligan exchange banter on the parapet of their Martello tower overlooking Dublin Bay. Everything speaks of sparkling life and wit; but all the undertones are of hostility, battle and betrayal. The brash usurper, Mulligan, is ever-mocking, ever on the attack. When his earnest English guest, Haines, speaks, he is too loud, too confident, too condescending with the Irish. An old milk-woman is servile, or rather apes servility, her tongue quick to please or placate. Caught among these voices, Stephen's is distinctively swift, deft, witty, but shot through with sadness and guilt. And it has another characteristic. He listens in silence to the by-play between Mulligan, Haines and the old milk-woman:

> She bows her old head to a voice that speaks to her loudly, her bonesetter, her medicineman; me she slights. To the voice that will shrive and oil for the grave all there is of her but her woman's unclean loins, of man's flesh made not in God's likeness, the serpent's prey. And to the loud voice that now bids her be silent with wondering unsteady eyes.

Stephen listens in silence, and his voice is silent. For he is talking to himself. And the great innovation of *Ulysses* emerges: the interior monologue. The device was not Joyce's invention, but with it he discovered wholly new ways of presenting personality in fiction: the apparently casual shiftings of a mind moved by wayward association, a stream of consciousness. Stephen's and Bloom's silent voices, their monologues, are made to sound like the direct communication of thought as it is being thought: spontaneous and immediate. Of course those monologues are subject to all Joyce's orderings within the economy of *Ulysses* (behind Stephen's thoughts about the milk-woman runs a *Portrait*-theme: Ireland, subservient to a Church, and to a State directed by foreign masters, ignores her would-be artist-redeemer: 'me she slights.'). The wonder is that these interior voices, puppets of Joyce's ingenious imagination, total artifice, can sound so totally natural.

Each of the inner voices has a distinctive note. Stephen's bookish habit of rapid allusion makes his the most difficult to catch in flight. Here, for example, he has just flinchingly spoken of his mother's death. Mulligan, impatiently rallying him, booms out 'Forget the moody brooding', and then drones a few lines of the Yeats poem he has casually invoked:

> And no more turn aside and brood
> Upon love's bitter mystery
> For Fergus rules the brazen cars.

Yeats's words combine with an earlier, biblical vision of the sea as a 'bowl of bitter waters', linked in Stephen's quick, wounded mind with a bowl at his dying mother's bedside, and now linked with further fragments from the same Yeats poem:

> Woodshadows floated silently by through the morning peace from the stairhead seaward where he gazed. Inshore and farther out the mirror of water whitened, spurned by lightshod hurrying feet. White breast of the dim sea. The twining stresses, two by two. A hand plucking the harpstrings merging their twining chords. Wavewhite wedded words shimmering on the dim tide.

A cloud began to cover the sun slowly, shadowing the bay in a deeper green. It lay behind him, a bowl of bitter waters. Fergus' song: I sang it alone in the house, holding down the long dark chords. Her door was open: she wanted to hear my music. Silent with awe and pity I went to her bedside. She was crying in her wretched bed. For those words, Stephen: love's bitter mystery.

Where now?

All the compacted richness of Joyce's text is here. All is artifice yet all remains natural and intense, and of an almost unbearable poignancy.

Bloom's inner voice is quite different. The tone and rhythms, plain and placid, are full of quirky stops and starts. More down to earth and concerned with the world outside himself than Stephen has yet learnt to be, Bloom's mental life, so modest, yet so rich in observation, richer really than Stephen's, in effect lies at the heart of *Ulysses*. At this point in the novel, he thinks about the woman in the Maternity Hospital:

> Three days imagine groaning on a bed with a vinegared handkerchief round her forehead, her belly swollen out! Phew! Dreadful simply! Child's head too big: forceps. Doubled up inside her trying to butt its way out blindly, groping for the way out. Kill me that would. Lucky Molly got over hers lightly. They ought to invent something to stop that. Life with hard labour. Twilightsleep idea: queen Victoria was given that. Nine she had. A good layer. Old woman that lived in a shoe she had so many children. Suppose he was consumptive. Time someone thought about it instead of gassing about the what was it the pensive bosom of the silver effulgence. Flapdoodle to feed fools on. They could easily have big establishments. Whole thing quite painless out of all the taxes give every child born five quid at compound interest up to twentyone, five per cent is a hundred shillings and five tiresome pounds, multiply by twenty decimal system, encourage people to put by money save hundred and ten and a bit twentyone years want to work it out on paper come to a tidy sum, more than you think.
>
> Not stillborn of course. They are not even registered. Trouble for nothing.

This is a typical bit of Bloomery: his concern, relaxed but real, for the woman in childbirth; his woolly benevolence; his wit,

gentler than Stephen's but sharp enough, his patient commonsense; his tendency to get things slightly wrong (like his mathematics); his mind's habit of always wandering back to Molly, with here a fleeting memory of his dead child – all small fragments in the immensely detailed mosaic of Bloom's self that Joyce builds up, through his silent voice.

In the final episode comes sleepy Molly's marvellous hithering, thithering meditation. The ebb and flow of her unpunctuated, uninhibited musings on her past life and on the day's events sets the whole movement of *Ulysses* in a new perspective, and re-examines a lot of Dublin male posturing. Here, in the midst of her erotic memories, her mind slips back to her infant son, who had lived only eleven days; and then to Stephen, who has aroused vaguely maternal and very vaguely erotic instincts:

> I suppose I oughtnt to have buried him in that little woolly jacket I knitted crying as I was but give it to some poor child but I knew well Id never have another our 1st death too it was we were never the same since O Im not going to think myself into the glooms about that any more I wonder why he wouldnt stay the night I felt all the time it was somebody strange he brought in instead of roving around the city meeting God knows who nightwalkers and pickpockets his poor mother wouldnt like that if she was alive ruining himself for life perhaps. . . .

Molly's voice comes closest to simulating a true stream of consciousness, slipping from one association to another, apparently without any grammatical or syntactical hindrance. 'Penelope' is as highly structured as any of the other episodes, while still offering the brilliant illusion of direct contact with an almost asleep mind and an almost asleep speaker. This last voice in *Ulysses* leads naturally into what came next.

————

From 1920 Joyce had lived in Paris, maintaining, as surprised visitors often remarked, a high bourgeois style, choosing expensive apartments (frequently changed, in the family tradition), eating, and especially drinking, in fancy restaurants, offering generous hospitality to friends and guests. And why not? He now had some resources; various small grants had come his way, and from 1917 a large sum and then further amazingly large sums of money began to come to him from the remarkable Harriet Weaver, an English literary magazine editor with a private income who became his generous, and for a long time anonymous, patron.

But Joyce always lived far beyond his means, so he was never without money worries. *Ulysses* and its problems, including ruthless piracy in America, nagged away at him from first to last, but in the sixteen years or so that he worked on *Finnegans Wake*, much more serious difficulties arose in his life. His eyes, never strong, had begun to give out. Surgery for glaucoma was first performed in 1917, and over the next twenty years he had to suffer no fewer than twelve excruciating operations. By the late 1920s he could only read with great difficulty; so for the immense task he had set himself in his new book, he had to rely on a coterie of disciples willing to help this notably impatient and irascible master with his reading, and to take dictation of his writing.

A more intimately painful problem arose with his daughter, Lucia, who in her early twenties began to show signs of serious mental illness. She had a schizophrenic breakdown in 1932 and her parents struggled to save her. But after some very disturbing, sometimes violent, family scenes, hospitalization seemed the only possible recourse. Joyce suffered greatly.

He was also much troubled by the strongly negative reactions from many literary friends, including Miss Weaver herself, to his new experimental work. Extracts, known only, teasingly, as 'Work in Progress' until its eventual publication in 1939, had started to appear in avant-garde magazines in the early twenties. Although a cult of devoted admirers quickly developed, many writers important to Joyce did not hesitate to express their puzzlement and even alarm at what he was writing. More than once he thought of abandoning the project but, with extraordinary courage and energy, he always recovered and resumed his struggle to turn 'Work in Progress' at last into *Finnegans Wake*.

As *Ulysses*'s day ends, Molly Bloom lies beside her husband speaking sleepy words to herself. But *Finnegans Wake* is a night-book, a dream-book. Humphrey Chimpden Earwicker – HCE for short – lies fast asleep beside his wife, and what he has to say comes out in dream-speech. Joyce once explained to Harriet Weaver what he was up to: 'One great part of every human existence is passed in a state which can not be rendered sensible by the use of wideawake language, cutanddry grammar and goahead plot.' So his new deepsleep language is a compendious expansion and contraction of daytalk, a language unlike anything heard in fiction before. It pours into its words borrowings from all space and all time. English words climb macaronically in and out of other European languages, with bits and pieces added from all over the world. Puns build on half-puns, phrases and sentences build up in the same way. Behind one identifiable sentence others jostle for attention; popular songs (hundreds of them), ballads, hymns, prayers, snitches of this and snatches of that, submerged quotations from great writers, bald clichés from lesser ones climb on top of one another. The sentences themselves refuse to behave, will not stay in place, slither out of our grasp. That is Joyce's non-wideawake language and non-cutanddry grammar. Similarly, *Finnegans Wake*'s vestigial plot is non-goahead; in fact it is circular, as the last incomplete sentence of the book brings us round by 'a commodious vicus of recirculation' to the beginning again.

It is impossible to encapsulate the *Wake* as a story, but there *are* some recognizable characters. HCE is the central protagonist, or head-dreamer. A middle-aged Dubliner with a wife and three children, he is not unlike Leopold Bloom: non-Catholic, with a non-Irish name, he too is a bit of an outsider, and he too is engaged in small-time commerce, as landlord of a struggling pub on the outskirts of the city. Joyce, as usual, is writing on one level about ordinary people's ordinary lives. HCE has had a bad day in the pub and has gone to sleep drunk. Worries swim up in his dream: his uncertain feelings for his ageing wife, Anna Livia, his troubled dealings with one or both of his sons, Shem and Shaun; his inchoate incestuous interest, real or imagined, in his daughter, Isabel or Issy. And has he or hasn't he been involved in some obscure, perhaps homosexual misdemeanour in nearby Phoenix Park? Is some thunderous catastrophe looming?

That could be called a working approach to the story. But dreams are not straightforward; their plots will not stay in place either. Human identities shift and, as in the 'Circe' episode of *Ulysses*, objects take on slippery identities of their own. HCE and his family, it turns out, are not only universally representative, the bearers of every man's desires and guilts; they *become* countless other exemplars of man's inevitable rise and fall. So HCE shifts from being his own lowly self to inhabiting an even lowlier self: Tim Finnegan, a drunken builder's labourer. But he also becomes Finn McCool, the giant Irish hero who lies beside the river Liffey, watching the history of Ireland and the world – its past and its future – flow by; he becomes Ibsen's *Master Builder*, and Napoleon and many another great builder and destroyer of civilizations.

HCE, in fact, has hundreds of identities. For example, he can be not only a builder, Hod Cement and Edifices; but a director, Hotel and Creamery Establishment; or a businessman, Honour Commercio's Energy. He can be all of Dublin, Howth Castle and Environs; he is all fathers, Haveth Childers Everywhere, and in the end he is all men: Here Comes Everybody. His initials, we are told, appear ten thousand times within words or as acrostics in *Finnegans Wake* (though who's counting?).

*Finnegans Wake* creates or plays at creating a universal myth, and such a myth, Joyce decided, demanded a simulated universal language. Hence the basic difficulty everyone experiences with the book: the difficulty of learning that language. If *Ulysses* can occasionally be daunting, *Finnegans Wake* regularly has the reader in retreat, wondering whether there can ever be any adequate recompense for the effort required.

Here is the first full sentence of the book:

> Sir Tristram, violer d'amores, fr'over the short sea, had passencore rearrived from North Armorica on this side the scraggy isthmus of Europe Minor to wielderfight his penisolate war: nor had topsawyer's rocks by the stream Oconee exaggerated themselse to Laurens County's gorgios while they went doublin their mumper all the time: nor avoice from afire bellowsed mishe mishe to tauftauf thuartpeatrick: not yet, though venissoon after, had a kidscad buttended a bland old isaac: not yet, though all's fair in vanessy, were sosie sesthers wroth with twone nathandjoe.

At first this seems impenetrable. But after a few readings a murky sense emerges: the subject is Dublin's past. Allusions dodge about in space and time. For a start the reader should recognize Tristan and Isolde (the Irish Iseult); the first Earl of Howth (family name, Tristram); St Patrick at his missionary work, also St Peter (whose Church was founded on a pun); Parnell struggling politically with Isaac Butt (and Parnell's childhood nickname, Butthead); the biblical Esau and Jacob; Dublin's Jonathan Swift, with his first name transposed, and Swift's women friends, Vanessa and Stella. The Peninsular War is there, and a town in Georgia, USA founded by a Dubliner named Sawyer, with a nod to Mark Twain. There are various obvious and less obvious other puns to catch, and it helps to know and recognize the French for not yet (*pas encore*) and twin (*sosie*), the Italian for whirlpool (*gorgo*), the German for fight again (*wiederfechten*) and baptize (*taufen*), the Latin for mount up (*exaggerare*) and the Greek for neck (*isthmos*).

*Ulysses* is a kind of joyful lesson, full of exuberant games through which Joyce teaches the reader how to read his book, offering the pupil plentiful rewards for attention on page after page. True, there are ambiguities, puzzles, mysteries, even a few impenetrable private jokes in *Ulysses*, but in the end we can say we have pretty well understood it, got most of the answers. *Finnegans Wake*, on the other hand, gives us many schoolbagsworth of homework that we know we'll never get done, despite all the help from teachers – expositors and interpreters – who have supplied cribs of one sort or another.

Yet with perseverance and patience the rewards can still be plentiful. Serious themes gradually become clearer; there are wonderfully extended jokes and ribaldries, and unexpected, startlingly beautiful lyric passages sing out. Yet always there are difficulties, so a note on tactics seems appropriate. The best approach is to skip along the text until something immediately attractive appears, then plunge in, after all it is a cyclical book so you can begin anywhere. Ignore the opening page and its Greek for neck and go straight to page eight and find 'This the way to the museyroom. Mind your hats goan in!' and *read it out loud* (always a good move with Joyce). Immediately his voice brings clarities; that ear is available again, with all its colloquial strength. In fact, a great part of *Finnegans Wake* is underpinned by the rhythms of everyday Dublin speech; for instance, the two washerwomen on the banks of the Liffey talk about HCE and his wife Anna Livia. Read aloud, the passage becomes clear enough; another lively indictment of HCE is under way. (What *did* he do in the Phoenix Park?)

0

tell me all about

Anna Livia! I want to hear all

about Anna Livia. Well, you know Anna Livia? Yes, of course, we all know Anna Livia. Tell me all. Tell me now. You'll die when you hear. Well, you know, when the old cheb went futt and did what you know. Yes, I know, go on. Wash quit and don't be dabbling. Tuck up your sleeves and loosen your talktapes. And don't butt me — hike! — when you bend. Or whatever it was they threed to make out he thried to two in the Fiendish park. He's an awful old reppe. Look at the shirt of him! Look at the dirt of it! He has all my water black on me. And it steeping and stuping since this time last wik. How many goes is it I wonder I washed it? I know by heart the places he likes to saale, duddurty devil! Scorching my hand and starving my famine to make his private linen public. Wallop it well with your battle and clean it. My wrists are wrusty rubbing the mouldaw stains.

Joyce has punningly inserted the names of twelve more-or-less obscure rivers: the Repe, the Upa, the Stupia, the Saale, the Moldau, and so on, into these otherwise pellucid rivery lines. Hundreds more rivers will swim up in the subsequent text. Is there a touch of the manic here? Or of the arbitrary and, ultimately, of the laborious? Never mind; the chapter careers superbly on, sustained in the washerwomen's happy blather: 'O, the roughty old rappe! Minxing marriage and making loof. . . . And the cut of him! And the strut of him! How he used to hold his head as high as a howeth. . . .' Or try this cheerful

Shem-portrait, pleasantly reminiscent of pictures of Joyce himself in middle-age:

> Putting truth and untruth together a shot may be made at what this hybrid actually was like to look at.
>
> Shem's bodily getup, it seems, included an adze of a skull, an eight of a larkseye, the whoel of a nose, one numb arm up a sleeve, fortytwo hairs off his uncrown, eighteen to his mock lip, a trio of barbels from his megageg chin (sowman's son), the wrong shoulder higher than the right, all ears, an artificial tongue with a natural curl, not a foot to stand on, a handful of thumbs, a blind stomach, a deaf heart, a loose liver, two fifths of two buttocks. . . .

And a last suggestion: quite a few passages in the *Wake* can with advantage be *sung*. For instance, HCE and Anna Livia are lying in bed together, and their son, Shem takes to disrespectful Father Prout-like verse to picture their embraces. The recommended tune to sing this paragraph to is 'Shandon Bells', a Cork song, but the overtones are Dublinish:

> When I turn meoptics, from suchurban prospects, 'tis my filial's bosom, doth behold with pride, that pontificator, and circumvallator, with his dam night garrulous, slipt by his side. Ann alive, the lisp of her, 'twould grig mountains whisper her, and the bergs of Iceland melt in waves of fire, and her spoon-me-spondees, and her dirckle-me-ondenees, make the Rageous Ossean, kneel and quaff a lyre! If Dann's dane, Ann's dirty, if he's plane she's purty, if he's fane, she's flirty, with her auburnt streams and her coy cajoleries, and her dabblin drolleries, for to rouse his rudderup, or to drench his dreams. If hot Hammurabi, or cowld Clesiastes, could espy her pranklings, they'd burst bounds agin, and renounce their ruings, and denounce their doings, for river and iver, and a night. Amin!

If we pursue the musical note, *Finnegans Wake* becomes a prolonged set of variations on a repeated theme. As the book's opening phrase is 'riverrun, past Eve and Adam's' the theme appears to be the Fall of Man, Original Sin. But Joyce takes us far beyond the specifically biblical or Christian formulation. He uses his multifarious versions of the rise and inevitable fall of man and his world as metaphor for the common human sense of psychic distress. Temptation, uncertainty, and above all, guilt – sensations already examined *chez* Bloom and Stephen – are now most vividly alive in the *Wake*'s unconscious, anarchic dream-world. These cyclical confrontations with man's nature constitute Joyce's serious central theme. Recalling his 'moral history' in *Dubliners*, his attention to the 'uncreated conscience' in *Portrait*, and the appeal for a moral understanding that lies at the heart of what Stephen, Molly, and above all, Bloom, are made to say for themselves in *Ulysses*, there is nothing incongruous in stressing the seriousness of Joyce's subject in *Finnegans Wake*.

But Adam or no Adam, falls are irremediably comic, as every clown knows. So Joyce's archetypal version of man's rise and fall is a raucous Dublin street-song about drunk Tim Finnegan climbing a ladder with his hod of bricks. Tim falls from his ladder and breaks his skull and, thought to be dead, is carried off to his wake, tied up in a nice clean sheet. At the wake rows and ructions soon begin, and some drunken bowsy flings a noggin of whiskey that scatters over Tim. Tim revives – 'See how he rises' – and as he drinks and swears, the cycle begins all over again. All men are Finnegans. Joyce didn't write the song, but it has a Joycean air about it, a Joycean voice, so there's lots of fun in *Finnegans Wake*.

---

His art thrived on dichotomies, doublings, the fusings of opposites. So it is no surprise that Joyce's letters and biographies present a personality full of contradictions. Looked at objectively, he can seem a quite unattractive man: a prig, a bit of a snob, a timid lecher, often a souse. A relentless borrower and shameless exploiter of family and friends, he was endlessly self-pitying and pettily contentious. He avidly sought out treachery and betrayals, and lovingly cherished a grudge.

Not all these vices are totally unsympathetic of course, but in any case we can fuse that cold indictment with his warm virtues: his delight in good fellowship, his engaging high spirits, his sudden generosities, and above all his consuming love for Nora and their children. And his courage; near the end of his life he wrote to his son, 'My eyes are tired. For more than half a century they've been staring into nothingness and finding a beautiful nothing.' But such despondency was rare in Joyce. What comes across in his late letters, for example, is a formidable driving will, fighting in 1940 (the last full year of his life) to withstand a succession of fierce personal blows, both public and private. The reception of *Finnegans Wake* was probably the worst of them. He had hoped with this book to make his peace with the world, and the thinness of response was a bitter disappointment.

Literature for Joyce ultimately meant festive comedy, the classic art of understanding and reconciliation. His later life, turbulent though it often was, also reflected a search for reconciliation. He wanted to make peace with his father in Dublin, and to make peace with Dublin itself. He grew progressively fonder of his rascally old parent, remorseful about not visiting him, then grief-stricken when the old man died in December, 1931. It happened that his own grandson, Stephen James Joyce, was born only a few weeks afterwards, and Joyce, briefly a poet again, wrote a short tense lyric, 'Ecce Puer' about that death and this birth. The poem ends:

> A child is sleeping:
> An old man gone.
> O, father forsaken,
> Forgive your son!

His own forgiveness of his native city had come quickly enough. At twenty-five Joyce was already telling his sceptical brother that the Irish were 'the most intelligent, most spiritual, and most civilised people in Europe'. But a reciprocal pardon took its time in coming, and lapses in his large-hearted tolerance inevitably erupted:

> This lovely land that always sent
> Her writers into banishment

was only one of several later begrudgings. Yet, as imagination and memory mingled, Joyce's obsession with Dublin grew touchingly close to devotion. He had got to the heart of Dublin after all. An acquaintance asked him if he would ever consider returning to Ireland. Joyce's response, 'Have I ever left it?'

Bernard McCabe *February 1993*     21

# DUBLINERS

We arranged to go along the Wharf Road until we came to the ships, then to cross in the ferryboat and walk out to see the Pigeon House. Leo Dillon was afraid we might meet Father Butler or some one out of the college; but Mahoney asked, very sensibly, what would Father Butler be doing out at the Pigeon House.

*From* 'An Encounter'

*Opposite* and *below:* the Pigeon House Generating Station

*Dubliners*

That night I slept badly. In the morning I was first-comer to the bridge as I lived nearest. I hid my books in the long grass near the ashpit at the end of the garden where nobody ever came and hurried along the canal bank. It was a mild sunny morning in the first week of June. I sat up on the coping of the bridge admiring my frail canvas shoes which I had diligently pipeclayed overnight and watching the docile horses pulling a tramload of business people up the hill. All the branches of the tall trees which lined the mall were gay with little light green leaves and the sunlight slanted through them on to the water. The granite stone of the bridge was beginning to be warm and I began to pat it with my hands in time to an air in my head. I was very happy.

*From* 'An Encounter'

The Grand Canal

North Richmond Street, being blind, was a quiet street except at the hour when the Christian Brothers' School set the boys free. An uninhabited house of two storeys stood at the blind end, detached from its neighbours in a square ground. The other houses of the street, conscious of decent lives within them, gazed at one another with brown imperturbable faces.

*From* 'Araby'

27

*Dubliners*

Lenehan walked as far as the Shelbourne Hotel where he halted and waited. After waiting for a little time he saw them coming towards him and, when they turned to the right, he followed them, stepping lightly in his white shoes, down one side of Merrion Square. As he walked on slowly, timing his pace to theirs, he watched Corley's head which turned at every moment towards the young woman's face like a big ball revolving on a pivot. He kept the pair in view until he had seen them climbing the stairs of the Donnybrook tram; then he turned about and went back the way he had come.

Now that he was alone his face looked older. His gaiety seemed to forsake him, and, as he came by the railings of the Duke's Lawn, he allowed his hand to run along them. The air which the harpist had played began to control his movements. His softly padded feet played the melody while his fingers swept a scale of variations idly along the railings after each group of notes.

He walked listlessly round Stephen's Green and then down Grafton Street. Though his eyes took note of many elements of the crowd through which he passed they did so morosely. He found trivial all that was meant to charm him and did not answer the glances which invited him to be bold.

*From 'Two Gallants'*

*Left:* the Shelbourne Hotel
*Right:* St Stephen's Green

29

*Dubliners*

Little Chandler quickened his pace. For the first time in his life he felt himself superior to the people he passed. For the first time his soul revolted against the dull inelegance of Capel Street. There was no doubt about it: if you wanted to succeed you had to go away. You could do nothing in Dublin. As he crossed Grattan Bridge he looked down the river towards the lower quays and pitied the poor stunted houses. They seemed to him a band of tramps, huddled together along the river-banks, their old coats covered with dust and soot stupefied by the panorama of sunset and waiting for the first chill of night to bid them arise, shake themselves and begone. He wondered whether he could write a poem to express his idea. Perhaps Gallaher might be able to get it into some London paper for him. Could he write something original? He was not sure what idea he wished to express but the thought that a poetic moment had touched him took life within him like an infant hope. He stepped onward bravely.

*From 'A Little Cloud'*

Looking out from Grattan Bridge

*Above* and *right:* Grattan Bridge and the lower quays

33

*Dubliners*

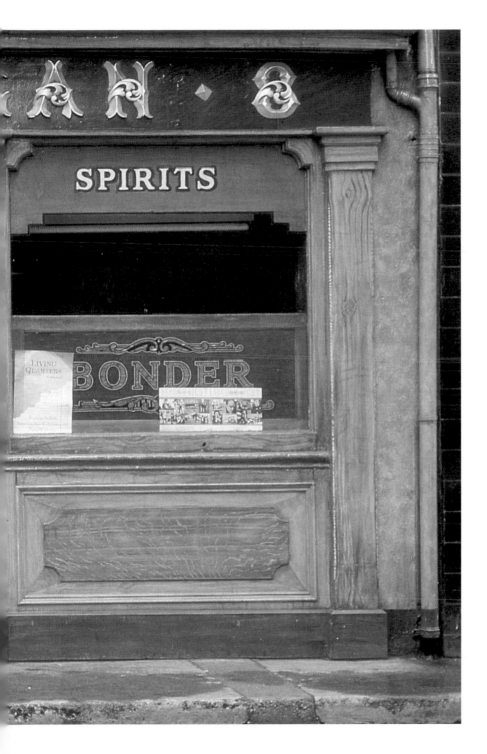

Weathers made them all have just one little tincture at his expense and promised to meet them later on at Mulligan's in Poolbeg Street.

When the Scotch House closed they went round to Mulligan's. They went into the parlour at the back and O'Halloran ordered small hot specials all round. They were all beginning to feel mellow. Farrington was just standing another round when Weathers came back. Much to Farrington's relief he drank a glass of bitter this time. Funds were running low but they had enough to keep them going.

*From* 'Counterparts'

*Left* and *above:* Mulligan's in Poolbeg Street

35

It was after nine o'clock when he left the shop. The night was cold and gloomy. He entered the park by the first gate and walked along under the gaunt trees. He walked through the bleak alleys where they had walked four years before. She seemed to be near him in the darkness.

At moments he seemed to feel her voice touch his ear, her hand touch his. He stood still to listen. Why had he withheld life from her? Why had he sentenced her to death? He felt his moral nature falling to pieces.

*From* 'A Painful Case'

Phoenix Park

When he gained the crest of the Magazine Hill he halted and looked along the river towards Dublin, the lights of which burned redly and hospitably in the cold night. He looked down the slope and, at the base, in the shadow of the wall of the park, he saw some human figures lying. Those venal and furtive loves filled him with despair. He gnawed the rectitude of his life; he felt that he had been outcast from life's feast. One human being had seemed to love him and he had denied her life and happiness: he had sentenced her to ignominy, a death of shame. He knew that the prostrate creatures down by the wall were watching him and wished him gone. No one wanted him; he was outcast from life's feast.

*From* 'A Painful Case'

*Dubliners*

39

Beyond the river he saw a goods train winding out of Kingsbridge Station, like a worm with a fiery head winding through the darkness, obstinately and laboriously. It passed slowly out of sight; but still he heard in his ears the laborious drone of the engine reiterating the syllables of her name.

*From* 'A Painful Case'

Kingsbridge Station, renamed Heuston Station

*Dubliners*

A few light taps upon the pane made him turn to the window. It had begun to snow again. He watched sleepily the flakes, silver and dark, falling obliquely against the lamplight. The time had come for him to set out on his journey westward. Yes, the newspapers were right: snow was general all over Ireland. It was falling on every part of the dark central plain, on the treeless hills, falling softly upon the Bog of Allen and, farther westward, softly falling into the dark mutinous Shannon waves. It was falling, too, upon every part of the lonely churchyard on the hill where Michael Furey lay buried. It lay thickly drifted on the crooked crosses and headstones, on the spears of the little gate, on the barren thorns. His soul swooned slowly as he heard the snow falling faintly through the universe and faintly falling, like the descent of their last end, upon all the living and the dead.

*From* 'The Dead'

The Bog of Allen

*Dubliners*

# POEMS

Strings in the earth and air
   Make music sweet;
Strings by the river where
   The willows meet.

There's music along the river
   For Love wanders there,
Pale flowers on his mantle,
   Dark leaves on his hair.

All softly playing,
   With head to the music bent,
And fingers straying
   Upon an instrument.

The River Liffey

*Poems*

### She Weeps Over Rahoon

Rain on Rahoon falls softly, softly falling,
Where my dark lover lies.
Sad is his voice that calls me, sadly calling,
At grey moonrise.

Love, hear thou
How soft, how sad his voice is ever calling,
Ever unanswered, and the dark rain falling,
Then as now.

Dark too our hearts, O love, shall lie and cold
As his sad heart has lain
Under the moongrey nettles, the black mould
And muttering rain.

The burial place of Michael Bodkin, model for
Michael Furey in 'The Dead', Rahoon, Galway

All day I hear the noise of waters
    Making moan,
Sad as the sea-bird is, when going
    Forth alone,
He hears the winds cry to the waters'
    Monotone.

The grey winds, the cold winds are blowing
    Where I go.
I hear the noise of many waters
    Far below.
All day, all night, I hear them flowing
    To and fro.

The sea at Sandycove

49

# A PORTRAIT OF THE ARTIST AS A YOUNG MAN

It would be better to be in the studyhall than out there in the cold. The sky was pale and cold but there were lights in the castle. He wondered from which window Hamilton Rowan had thrown his hat on the haha and had there been flowerbeds at that time under the windows. One day when he had been called to the castle the butler had shown him the marks of the soldiers' slugs in the wood of the door and had given him a piece of shortbread that the community ate. It was nice and warm to see the lights in the castle. It was like something in a book.

*Left* and *below:* Clongowes Wood College, Co. Kildare

He opened the geography to study the lesson; but he could not learn the names of places in America. Still they were all different places that had those different names. They were all in different countries and the countries were in continents and the continents were in the world and the world was in the universe.

He turned to the flyleaf of the geography and read what he had written there: himself, his name and where he was.

Stephen Dedalus
Class of Elements
Clongowes Wood College
Sallins
County Kildare
Ireland
Europe
The World
The Universe

That was in his writing: and Fleming one night for a cod had written on the opposite page:

Stephen Dedalus is my name,
Ireland is my nation.
Clongowes is my dwellingplace
And heaven my expectation.

The study hall, Clongowes Wood College

*A Portrait of the Artist as a Young Man*

*A Portrait of the Artist as a Young Man*

It was easy what he had to do. All he had to do was when the dinner was over and he came out in his turn to go on walking but not out to the corridor but up the staircase on the right that led to the castle. He had nothing to do but that: to turn to the right and walk fast up the staircase and in half a minute he would be in the low dark narrow corridor that led through the castle to the rector's room.

The prefect of the chapel prayed above his head and his memory knew the responses:

O Lord, open our lips
And our mouths shall announce Thy praise.
Incline unto our aid, O God!
O Lord, make haste to help us!

There was a cold night smell in the chapel. But it was a holy smell. It was not like the smell of the old peasants who knelt at the back of the chapel at Sunday mass. That was a smell of air and rain and turf and corduroy. But they were very holy peasants. They breathed behind him on his neck and sighed as they prayed.

*Left:* the approach to the rector's room
*Right:* the school chapel

55

They lived in Clane, a fellow said: there were little cottages there and he had seen a woman standing at the halfdoor of a cottage with a child in her arms, as the cars had come past from Sallins. It would be lovely to sleep for one night in that cottage before the fire of smoking turf, in the dark lit by the fire, in the warm dark, breathing the smell of the peasants, air and rain and turf and corduroy. But, O, the road there between the trees was dark! You would be lost in the dark. It made him afraid to think of how it was.

Cottages in Clane, near Sallins, Co. Kildare

*A Portrait of the Artist as a Young Man*

*A Portrait of the Artist as a Young Man*

*A Portrait of the Artist as a Young Man*

At Maryborough he fell asleep. When he awoke the train had passed out of Mallow and his father was stretched asleep on the other seat. The cold light of the dawn lay over the country, over the unpeopled fields and the closed cottages. The terror of sleep fascinated his mind as he watched the silent country or heard from time to time his father's deep breath or sudden sleepy movement.

Travelling from Cork to Mallow     59

*A Portrait of the Artist as a Young Man*

They drove in a jingle across Cork while it was still early morning and Stephen finished his sleep in a bedroom of the Victoria Hotel. The bright warm sunlight was streaming through the window and he could hear the din of traffic. His father was standing before the dressingtable, examining his hair and face and moustache with great care, craning his neck across the waterjug and drawing it back sideways to see the better. While he did so he sang softly to himself with quaint accent and phrasing:

> 'Tis youth and folly
> Makes young men marry,
> So here, my love, I'll
>     No longer stay.
> What can't be cured, sure,
> Must be injured, sure,
>     So I'll go to
>     Amerikay.
> . . .

The consciousness of the warm sunny city outside his window and the tender tremors with which his father's voice festooned the strange sad happy air, drove off all the mists of the night's ill humour from Stephen's brain. He got up quickly to dress and, when the song had ended, said:

– That's much prettier than any of your other *come-all-yous*.

St Finnbarr Cathedral and the banks of the river Lee, in Cork city

*A Portrait of the Artist as a Young Man*

61

He turned seaward from the road at Dollymount and as he passed on to the thin wooden bridge he felt the planks shaking with the tramp of heavily shod feet. A squad of Christian Brothers was on its way back from the Bull and had begun to pass, two by two, across the bridge. Soon the whole bridge was trembling and resounding. The uncouth faces passed him two by two, stained yellow or red or livid by the sea, and as he strove to look at them with ease and indifference, a faint stain of personal shame and commiseration rose to his own face. Angry with himself he tried to hide his face from their eyes by gazing down sideways into the shallow swirling water under the bridge but he still saw a reflection therein of their top-heavy silk hats, and humble tapelike collars and loosely hanging clerical clothes.

– Brother Hickey.
Brother Quaid.
Brother MacArdle.
Brother Keogh.

Their piety would be like their names, like their faces, like their clothes and it was idle for him to tell himself that their humble and contrite hearts, it might be, paid a far richer tribute of devotion than his had ever been, a gift tenfold more acceptable than his elaborate adoration.

The wooden bridge at Dollymount

*A Portrait of the Artist as a Young Man*

*A Portrait of the Artist as a Young Man*

*A Portrait of the Artist as a Young Man*

The grey block of Trinity on his left, set heavily in the city's ignorance like a great dull stone set in a cumbrous ring, pulled his mind downward; and while he was striving this way and that to free his feet from the fetters of the reformed conscience he came upon the droll statue of the national poet of Ireland.

He looked at it without anger: for, though sloth of the body and of the soul crept over it like unseen vermin, over the shuffling feet and up the folds of the cloak and around the servile head, it seemed humbly conscious of its indignity. It was a Firbolg in the borrowed cloak of a Milesian . . . .

Well, I started to walk and on I went and it was coming on night when I got into the Ballyhoura hills; that's better than ten miles from Kilmallock and there's a long lonely road after that. You wouldn't see the sign of a christian house along the road or hear a sound. It was pitch dark almost. Once or twice I stopped by the way under a bush to redden my pipe and only for the dew was thick I'd have stretched out there and slept. At last, after a bend of the road, I spied a little cottage with a light in the window. I went up and knocked at the door. A voice asked who was there and I answered I was over at the match in Buttevant and was walking back and that I'd be thankful for a glass of water. After a while a young woman opened the door and brought me out a big mug of milk. She was half undressed as if she was going to bed when I knocked and she had her hair hanging; and I thought by her figure and by something in the look of her eyes that she must be carrying a child. She kept me in talk a long while at the door and I thought it strange because her breast and her shoulders were bare. She asked me was I tired and would I like to stop the night there. She said she was all alone in the house and that her husband had gone that morning to Queenstown with her sister to see her off. And all the time she was talking, Stevie, she had her eyes fixed on my face and she stood so close to me I could hear her breathing. When I handed her back the mug at last she took my hand to draw me in over the threshold and said: *Come in and stay the night here. You've no call to be frightened. There's no one in it but ourselves. . . .* I didn't go in, Stevie. I thanked her and went on my way again, all in a fever. At the first bend of the road I looked back and she was standing at the door.

The Ballyhoura Hills, Co. Limerick

*A Portrait of the Artist as a Young Man*

*A Portrait of the Artist as a Young Man*

They had walked on towards the township of Pembroke and now, as they went on slowly along the avenues, the trees and the scattered lights in the villas soothed their minds. The air of wealth and repose diffused about them seemed to comfort their neediness. Behind a hedge of laurel a light glimmered in the window of a kitchen and the voice of a servant was heard singing as she sharpened knives. She sang, in short broken bars, *Rosie O'Grady*.

69

The rain fell faster. When they passed through the passage beside the royal Irish academy they found many students sheltering under the arcade of the library. Cranly, leaning against a pillar, was picking his teeth with a sharpened match, listening to some companions. Some girls stood near the entrance door.

The National Library

*A Portrait of the Artist as a Young Man*

Welcome, O life! I go to encounter for the millionth time the reality of experience and to forge in the smithy of my soul the uncreated conscience of my race.

27 April: Old father, old artificer, stand me now and ever in good stead.

Dublin 1904
Trieste 1914

Leaving Dublin

*A Portrait of the Artist as a Young Man*

*A Portrait of the Artist as a Young Man*

# ULYSSES

Stately, plump Buck Mulligan came from the stairhead, bearing a bowl of lather on which a mirror and a razor lay crossed. A yellow dressing-gown, ungirdled, was sustained gently behind him by the mild morning air. He held the bowl aloft and intoned:

   *– Introibo ad altare Dei.*

_____

*Left* and *below:* the Martello tower at Sandycove

Haines asked:

   – Do you pay rent for this tower?

   – Twelve quid, Buck Mulligan said.

   – To the secretary of state for war, Stephen added over his shoulder.

   They halted while Haines surveyed the tower and said at last:

   – Rather bleak in wintertime, I should say. Martello you call it?

   – Billy Pitt had them built, Buck Mulligan said, when the French were on the sea. But ours is the *omphalos*.

The Tower and its parapet

Stephen stood up and went over to the parapet. Leaning on it he looked down on the water and on the mailboat clearing the harbour mouth of Kingstown.

– Our mighty mother, Buck Mulligan said.

He turned abruptly his great searching eyes from the sea to Stephen's face.

– The aunt thinks you killed your mother, he said. That's why she won't let me have anything to do with you.

– Someone killed her, Stephen said gloomily.

– You could have knelt down, damn it, Kinch, when your dying mother asked you, Buck Mulligan said. I'm hyperborean as much as you. But to think of your mother begging you with her last breath to kneel down and pray for her. And you refused. There is something sinister in you . . .

————

They followed the winding path down to the creek . . . A young man clinging to a spur of rock near him moved slowly frogwise his green legs in the deep jelly of the water . . .

Stephen turned away.

– I'm going, Mulligan, he said.

– Give us that key, Kinch, Buck Mulligan said, to keep my chemise flat.

Stephen handed him the key. Buck Mulligan laid it across his heaped clothes.

– And twopence, he said, for a pint. Throw it there.

Stephen threw two pennies on the soft heap. Dressing, undressing. Buck Mulligan erect, with joined hands before him, said solemnly:

– He who stealeth from the poor lendeth to the Lord. Thus spake Zarathustra.

His plump body plunged.

The Forty Foot Hole

*Ulysses*

*Ulysses*

– You, Armstrong, Stephen said. What was the end of Pyrrhus?

– End of Pyrrhus, sir?

– I know, sir. Ask me, sir, Comyn said.

– Wait. You, Armstrong. Do you know anything about Pyrrhus?

A bag of figrolls lay snugly in Armstrong's satchel. He curled them between his palms at whiles and swallowed them softly. Crumbs adhered to the tissues of his lips. A sweetened boy's breath. Welloff people, proud that their eldest son was in the navy. Vico Road, Dalkey.

– Pyrrhus, sir? Pyrrhus, a pier.

All laughed. Mirthless high malicious laughter. Armstrong looked round at his classmates, silly glee in profile. In a moment they will laugh more loudly, aware of my lack of rule and of the fees their papas pay.

– Tell me now, Stephen said, poking the boy's shoulder with the book, what is a pier.

– A pier, sir, Armstrong said. A thing out in the waves. A kind of bridge. Kingstown pier, sir.

Some laughed again: mirthless but with meaning. Two in the back bench whispered. Yes. They knew: had never learned nor ever been innocent. All. With envy he watched their faces. Edith, Ethel, Gerty, Lily. Their likes: their breaths, too, sweetened with tea and jam, their bracelets tittering in the struggle.

– Kingstown pier, Stephen said. Yes, a disappointed bridge.

The words troubled their gaze.

*Left:* Joyce, like Stephen Dedalus, taught in this Dalkey house
*Below:* the pier at Kingstown, now Dun Laoghaire

*Ulysses*

Stephen closed his eyes to hear his boots crush crackling wrack and shells. You are walking through it howsomever. I am, a stride at a time. A very short space of time through very short times of space. Five, six: the *nacheinander*. Exactly: and that is the ineluctable modality of the audible. Open your eyes. No. Jesus! If I fell over a cliff that beetles o'er his base, fell through the *nebeneinander* ineluctably. I am getting on nicely in the dark. My ash sword hangs at my side. Tap with it: they do. My two feet in his boots are at the end of his legs, *nebeneinander*. Sounds solid: made by the mallet of *Los Demiurgos*. Am I walking into eternity along Sandymount strand?

Sandymount Strand

The grainy sand had gone from under his feet. His boots trod again a damp crackling mast, razorshells, squeaking pebbles, that on the unnumbered pebbles beats, wood sieved by the shipworm, lost Armada. Unwholesome sandflats waited to suck his treading soles, breathing upward sewage breath. He coasted them, walking warily. A porter-bottle stood up, stogged to its waist, in the cakey sand dough. A sentinel: isle of dreadful thirst. Broken hoops on the shore; at the land a maze of dark cunning nets; farther away chalkscrawled backdoors and on the higher beach a dryingline with two crucified shirts. Ringsend: wigwams of brown steersmen and master mariners. Human shells.

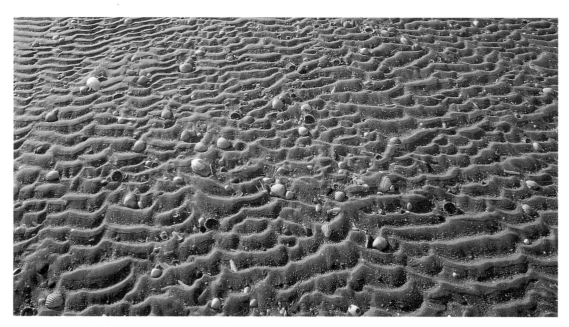

Their dog ambled about a bank of dwindling sand, trotting, sniffing on all sides. Looking for something lost in a past life. Suddenly he made off like a bounding hare, ears flung back, chasing the shadow of a lowskimming gull. The man's shrieked whistle struck his limp ears. He turned, bounded back, came nearer, trotted on twinkling shanks. On a field tenney a buck, trippant, proper, unattired. At the lacefringe of the tide he halted with stiff forehoofs, seawardpointed ears. His snout lifted barked at the wavenoise, herds of seamorse. They serpented towards his feet, curling, unfurling many crests, every ninth, breaking, plashing, from far, from farther out, waves and waves.

Sandymount Strand

*Ulysses*

*Ulysses*

Good puzzle would be cross Dublin without passing a pub.

85

*Ulysses*

By lorries along sir John Rogerson's Quay Mr Bloom walked soberly, past Windmill lane, Leask's the linseed crusher's, the postal telegraph office. Could have given that address too. And past the sailors' home. He turned from the morning noises of the quayside and walked through Lime street. By Brady's cottages a boy for the skins lolled, his bucket of offal linked, smoking a chewed fagbutt. A smaller girl with scars of eczema on her forehead eyed him, listlessly holding her battered caskhoop. Tell him if he smokes he won't grow. O let him! His life isn't such a bed of roses! Waiting outside pubs to bring da home. Come home to ma, da. Slack hour: won't be many there. He crossed Townsend street, passed the frowning face of Bethel. El, yes: house of: Aleph, Beth. And past Nichols' the undertaker's. At eleven it is. Time enough. Daresay Corny Kelleher bagged that job for O'Neill's.

*Left:* Sir John Rogerson's Quay seen from the North Wall

*Ulysses*

He had reached the open backdoor of All Hallows. Stepping into the porch he doffed his hat, took the card from his pocket and tucked it again behind the leather headband. . . .

The cold smell of sacred stone called him. He trod the worn steps, pushed the swingdoor and entered softly by the rere.

———

He saw the priest bend down and kiss the altar and then face about and bless all the people. All crossed themselves and stood up. Mr Bloom glanced about him and then stood up, looking over the risen hats. Stand up at the gospel of course. Then all settled down on their knees again and he sat quietly in his bench. The priest came down from the altar, holding the thing out from him, and he and the massboy answered each other in Latin. Then the priest knelt down and began to read off a card:

– O God, our refuge and our strength . . .

Mr Bloom put his face forward to catch the words. English. Throw them the bone. I remember slightly. How long since your last mass? Gloria and immaculate virgin. Joseph her spouse. Peter and Paul. More interesting if you understood what it was all about. Wonderful organisation certainly, goes like clockwork. Confession. Everyone wants to. Then I will tell you all. Penance. Punish me, please. Great weapon in their hands. More than doctor or solicitor. Woman dying to.

*Above* and *right:* St Andrew's, Westland Row, renamed by Joyce as All Hallows Church

*Ulysses*

The chemist turned back page after page. Sandy shrivelled smell he seems to have. Shrunken skull. And old. Quest for the philosopher's stone. The alchemists. Drugs age you after mental excitement. Lethargy then. Why? Reaction. A lifetime in a night. Gradually changes your character. Living all the day among herbs, ointments, disinfectants. All his alabaster lilypots. Mortar and pestle. Aq. Dist. Fol. Laur. Te Virid. Smell almost cure you like the dentist's doorbell.

92

Crossguns bridge: the royal canal.

Water rushed roaring through the sluices. A man stood on his dropping barge between clamps of turf. On the towpath by the lock a slacktethered horse. Aboard of the *Bugabu*.

Their eyes watched him. On the slow weedy waterway he had floated on his raft coastward over Ireland drawn by a haulage rope past beds of reeds, over slime, mudchoked bottles, carrion dogs. Athlone, Mullingar, Moyvalley, I could make a walking tour to see Milly by the canal. Or cycle down. Hire some old crock, safety. Wren had one the other day at the auction but a lady's. Developing waterways. James M'Cann's hobby to row me o'er the ferry. Cheaper transit. By easy stages. Houseboats. Camping out. Also hearses. To heaven by water. Perhaps I will without writing. Come as a surprise, Leixlip, Clonsilla. Dropping down, lock by lock to Dublin. With turf from the midland bogs. Salute. He lifted his brown straw hat, saluting Paddy Dignam.

The Royal Canal

The high railings of Prospects rippled past their gaze. Dark poplars, rare white forms. Forms more frequent, white shapes thronged amid the trees, white forms and fragments streaming by mutely, sustaining vain gestures on the air.

The gates glimmered in front: still open. Back to the world again. Enough of this place. Brings you a bit nearer every time. . . . Give you the creeps after a bit. I will appear to you after death. You will see my ghost after death. My ghost will haunt you after death. There is another world after death named hell. I do not like that other world she wrote. No more do I. Plenty to see and hear and feel yet. Feel live warm beings near you. Let them sleep in their maggoty beds. They are not going to get me this innings. Warm beds: warm fullblooded life.

Glasnevin Cemetery

*Ulysses*

*Ulysses*

Mr Bloom walked unheeded along his grove by saddened angels, crosses, broken pillars, family vaults, stone hopes praying with upcast eyes, old Ireland's hearts and hands. More sensible to spend the money on some charity for the living. Pray for the repose of the soul of. Does anybody really? Plant him and have done with him. Like down a coalshoot. Then lump them together to save time. All souls' day. Twentyseventh I'll be at his grave. Ten shillings for the gardener. He keeps it free of weeds. Old man himself. Bent down double with his shears clipping. Near death's door. Who passed away. Who departed this life. As if they did it of their own accord. Got the shove, all of them. Who kicked the bucket. More interesting if they told you what they were. So and so, wheelwright. I travelled for cork lino. I paid five shillings in the pound. Or a woman's with her saucepan. I cooked good Irish stew. Eulogy in a country churchyard it ought to be that poem of whose is it Wordsworth or Thomas Campbell. Entered into rest the protestants put it. Old Dr Murren's. The great physician called him home. Well it's God's acre for them. Nice country residence. Newly plastered and painted. Ideal spot to have a quiet smoke and read the *Church Times*. Marriage ads they never try to beautify. Rusty wreaths hung on knobs, garlands of bronzefoil. Better value that for the money. Still, the flowers are more poetical. The other gets rather tiresome, never withering. Expresses nothing. Immortelles.

He crossed under Tommy Moore's roguish finger. They did right to put him up over a urinal: meeting of the waters. Ought to be places for women. Running into cakeshops. Settle my hat straight.

His heart astir he pushed in the door of the Burton restaurant. Stink gripped his trembling breath: pungent meatjuice, slop of greens. See the animals feed.

Men, men, men.

Perched on high stools by the bar, hats shoved back, at the tables calling for more bread no charge, swilling, wolfing gobfuls of sloppy food, their eyes bulging, wiping wetted moustaches. A pallid suetfaced young man polished his tumbler knife fork and spoon with his napkin. New set of microbes. A man with an infant's saucestained napkin tucked round him shovelled gurgling soup down his gullet. A man spitting back on his plate: halfmasticated gristle: no teeth to chewchewchew it. Chump chop from the grill. Bolting to get it over. Sad booser's eyes. Bitten off more than he can chew. Am I like that?

*Left:* Tom Moore's statue
*Right:* midday in a Dublin cafe

*Ulysses*

As he set foot on O'Connell bridge a puffball of smoke plumed up from the parapet. Brewery barge with export stout. England. Sea air sours it, I heard. Be interesting some day get a pass through Hancock to see the brewery. Regular world in itself. Vats of porter, wonderful.

*Ulysses*

*Ulysses*

*Left:* Stephen on the reading room in the National Library

Coffined thoughts around me, in mummycases, embalmed in spice of words. Thoth, god of libraries, a birdgod, moonycrowned. And I heard the voice of that Egyptian highpriest. *In painted chambers loaded with tilebooks.*

————

Mr Bloom came to Kildare Street. First I must. Library.

Straw hat in sunlight. Tan shoes. Turnedup trousers. It is. It is.

His heart quopped softly. To the right. Museum . . . quiet there. Safe in a minute.

No, didn't see me. After two. Just at the gate.

My heart!

IIis eyes beating looked steadfastly at cream curves of stone. Sir Thomas Deane was the Greek architecture.

Look for something I.

His hasty hand went quick into a pocket, took out, read unfolded Agendath Netaim. Where did I?

Busy looking for.

He thrust back quickly Agendath.

Afternoon she said.

I am looking for that. Yes, that. Try all pockets. Handker. *Freeman.* Where did I? Ah, yes. Trousers. Purse. Potato. Where did I?

Hurry. Walk quietly. Moment more. My heart.

His hand looking for the where did I put found in his hip pocket soap lotion have to call tepid paper stuck. Ah, soap there! Yes. Gate.

Safe!

*Right:* the entrance to the National Museum, where Leopold Bloom avoids an encounter with Blazes Boylan

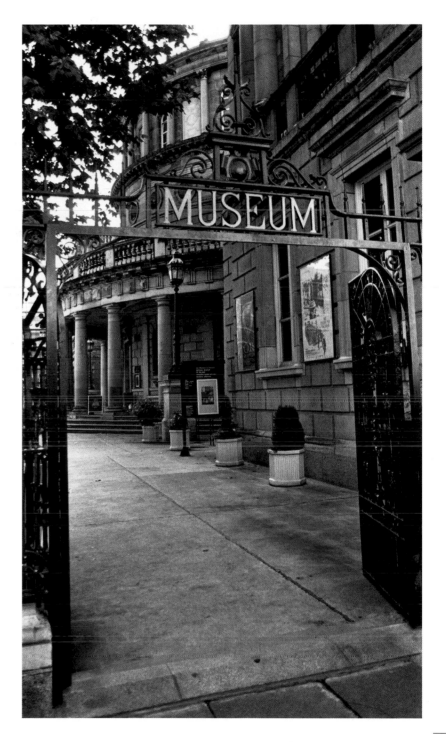

He entered Davy Byrne's. Moral pub. He doesn't chat. Stands a drink now and then. But in leapyear once in four. Cashed a cheque for me once.

What will I take now? He drew his watch. Let me see now. Shandy-gaff?

– Hellow, Bloom! Nosey Flynn said from his nook.

– Hello, Flynn.

– How's things?

– Tiptop . . . Let me see. I'll take a glass of burgundy and . . . let me see.

Sardines on the shelves. Almost taste them by looking. Sandwich? Ham and his descendants mustered and bred there. Potted meats. What is home without Plumtree's potted meat? Incomplete. What a stupid ad!

*Left* and *opposite:* Davy Byrne's today

– How interesting! a refined accent said in the gloom.

– Yes, sir, Ned Lambert said heartily. We are standing in the historic council chamber of saint Mary's abbey where silken Thomas proclaimed himself a rebel in 1534. That is the most historic spot in all Dublin. . . . Ned Lambert cracked his fingers in the air.

– God, he cried. I forgot to tell him that one about the earl of Kildare after he set fire to Cashel cathedral. You know that one? *I'm bloody sorry I did it*, says he, *but I declare to God I thought the archbishop was inside*. He mightn't like it, though. What? God, I'll tell him anyhow. That was the great earl, the Fitzgerald Mor. Hot members they were all of them, the Geraldines.

*Above:* St Mary's Abbey in Meetinghouse Lane

– What are you doing here, Stephen.

Dilly's high shoulders and shabby dress.

Shut the book quick. Don't let see.

– What are you doing? Stephen said.

A Stuart face of nonesuch Charles, lank locks falling at its sides. It glowed as she crouched feeding the fire with broken boots. I told her of Paris. Late lieabed under a quilt of old overcoats, fingering a pinchbeck bracelet, Dan Kelly's token. *Nebrakada femininum.*

– What have you there? Stephen asked.

– I bought it from the other cart for a penny, Dilly said, laughing nervously. Is it any good?

My eyes they say she has. Do others see me so? Quick, far and daring. Shadow of my mind.

He took the coverless book from her hand. Chardenal's French primer.

– What did you buy that for? he asked. To learn French?

She nodded, reddening and closing tight her lips.

Show no surprise. Quite natural.

– Here, Stephen said. It's all right. Mind Maggy doesn't pawn it on you. I suppose all my books are gone.

– Some, Dilly said. We had to.

She is drowning. Agenbite. Save her. Agenbite. All against us.

Bookstall near Merchant's Arch

*Ulysses*

*Ulysses*

At the Howth road stop Father Conmee alighted, was saluted by the conductor and saluted in his turn.

The Malahide road was quiet. It pleased Father Conmee, road and name. The joybells were ringing in gay Malahide. Lord Talbot de Malahide, immediate hereditary lord admiral of Malahide and the seas adjoining. Then came the call to arms and she was maid, wife and widow in one day. Those were oldworldish days, loyal times in joyous townlands, old times in the barony.

Father Conmee, walking, thought of his little book *Old Times in the Barony* and of the book that might be written about jesuit houses and of Mary Rochfort, daughter of lord Molesworth, first countess of Belvedere.

Malahide Castle, Co. Dublin

*Ulysses*

– I know, Mr Dedalus said, nodding. Poor old bockedy Ben! He's always doing a good turn for someone. Hold hard!

He put on his glasses and gazed towards the metal bridge an instant.

– There he is, by God, he said, arse and pockets.

Ben Dollard's loose blue cutaway and square hat above large slops crossed the quay in full gait from the metal bridge. He came towards them at an amble, scratching actively behind his coattails.

As he came near Mr Dedalus greeted:

– Hold that fellow with the bad trousers.

– Hold him now, Ben Dollard said.

Mr Dedalus eyed with cold wandering scorn various points of Ben Dollard's figure. Then, turning to Father Cowley with a nod, he muttered sneeringly:

– That's a pretty garment, isn't it, for a summer's day?

– Why, God eternally curse your soul, Ben Dollard growled furiously, I threw out more clothes in my time than you ever saw.

The Metal Bridge, or Halfpenny Bridge, across the Liffey

*Ulysses*

*Overleaf:*

The cavalcade passed out by the lower gate of Phoenix Park saluted by obsequious policemen and proceeded past Kingsbridge along the northern quays. The viceroy was most cordially greeted on his way through the metropolis. At Bloody bridge Mr Thomas Kernan beyond the river greeted him vainly from afar. Between Queen's and Whitworth bridges Lord Dudley's viceregal carriages passed and were unsaluted by Mr Dudley White, B. L., M. A., who stood on Arran Quay outside Mrs M. E. White's, the pawnbroker's, at the corner of Arran street west stroking his nose with his forefinger, undecided whether he should arrive at Phibsborough more quickly by a triple change of tram or by hailing a car or on foot through Smithfield, Constitution hill and Broadstone terminus. In the porch of Four Courts Richie Goulding with his costsbag of Goulding, Collis and Ward saw him with surprise. Past Richmond bridge at the doorstep of the office of Reuben J. Dodd, solicitor, agent for the Patriotic Insurance Company, an elderly female about to enter changed her plan and retracing her steps by King's windows smiled credulously on the representative of His Majesty.

*Overleaf:* 'A Pisgah Sight of Dublin'

– Are you a strict t. t.? says Joe.

– Not taking anything between drinks, says I.

– What about paying our respects to our friend? says Joe.

– Who? says I. Sure, he's in John of God's off his head, poor man.

– Drinking his own stuff? says Joe.

– Ay, says I. Whisky and water on the brain.

– Come around to Barney Kiernan's, says Joe. I want to see the citizen.

– Barney mavourneen's be it, says I.

Barney Kiernan's pub is gone forever, but Mulligan's survives

Hello. Where off to? Something to eat? I too was just. In here. What, Ormond? Best value in Dublin. Is that so? Dining-room. Sit tight there. See, not be seen. I think I'll join you. Come on. Richie led on. Bloom followed bag. Dinner fit for a prince.

Miss Douce reached high to take a flagon, stretching her satin arm, her bust, that all but burst, so high.

Life those chaps out there must have, stuck in the same spot. Irish Lights board. Penance for their sins. Coastguards too. Rocket and breeches buoy and lifeboat. Day we went out for the pleasure cruise in the Erin's King, throwing them the sack of old papers.

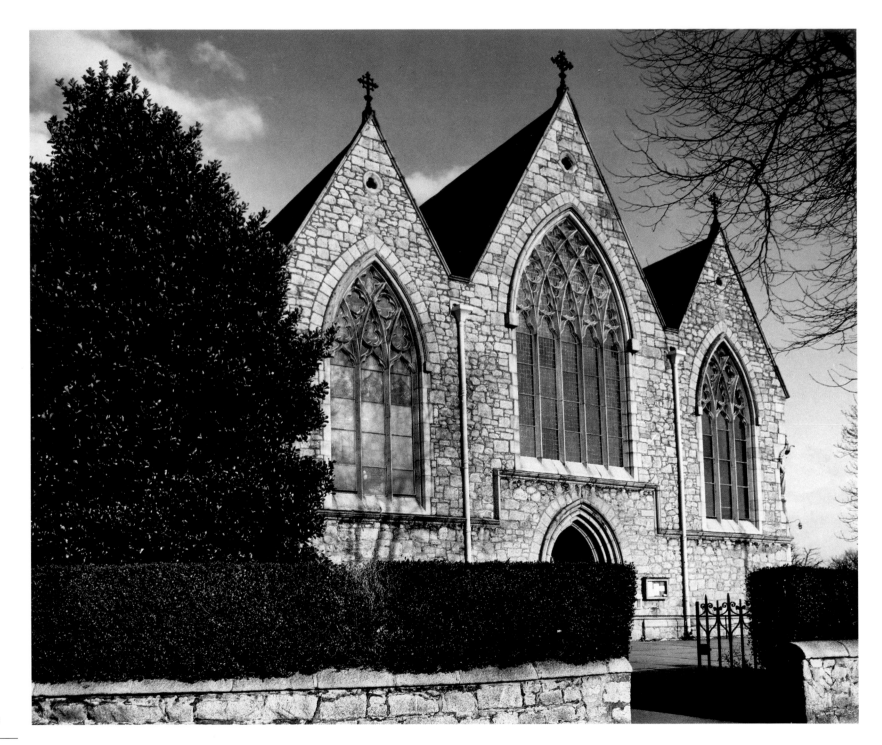

*Ulysses*

The summer evening had begun to fold the world in its mysterious embrace. Far away in the west the sun was setting

*Left:* Our Lady Star of the Sea at Sandymount
*Below:* Howth Head

and the last glow of all too fleeting day lingered lovingly on sea and strand, on the proud promontory of dear old Howth guarding as ever the waters of the bay, on the weedgrown rocks along Sandymount shore and, last but not

least, on the quiet church whence there streamed forth at times upon the stillness the voice of prayer to her who is in her pure radiance a beacon ever to the stormtossed heart of man, Mary, star of the sea.

*Ulysses*

And whiles they spake the door of the castle was opened and there nighed them a mickle noise as of many that sat there at meat. And there came against the place as they stood a young learning knight yclept Dixon. And the traveller Leopold was couth to him. . . . And the traveller Leopold went into the castle for to rest him for a space being sore of limb after many marches environing in divers lands and sometimes venery.

———————

BLOOM: Fish and taters. N. g. Ah! (*He disappears into Olhousen's, the pork butcher's, under the downcoming rollshutter. A few moments later he emerges from under the shutter, puffing Poldy, blowing Bloohoom. In each hand he holds a parcel, one containing a lukewarm pig's crubeen, the other a cold sheep's trotter, sprinkled with wholepepper. He gasps, standing upright. Then bending to one side he presses a parcel against his rib and groans.*)
BLOOM: Stitch in my side. Why did I run?

*Left:* the hospital where young Dixon is a student
*Right:* Olhousen's the pork butcher's, like Sweny's the chemist's and Nichols' the undertakers, is still going strong

*Ulysses*

BLOOM: *(In an oatmeal sporting suit, a sprig of woodbine in the lapel, tony buff shirt, shepherd's plaid Saint Andrew's cross scarftie, white spats, fawn dustcoat on his arm, tawny red brogues, fieldglasses in bandolier and a grey billycock hat)* Do you remember a long long time, years and years ago, just after Milly, Marionette we called her, was weaned when we all went together to Fairyhouse races, was it?

MRS BREEN: *(In smart Saxe tailormade, white velours hat and spider veil)* Leopardstown.

BLOOM: I mean, Leopardstown. And Molly won seven shillings on a three year old named Nevertell and coming home along by Foxrock in that old five-seater shanderadan of a waggonette you were in your heyday then and you had on that new hat of white velours with a surround of molefur that Mrs Hayes advised you to buy because it was marked down to nineteen and eleven, a bit of wire and an old rag of velveteen, and I'll lay you what you like she did it on purpose . . .

Leopardstown races

THE WATERFALL:
Poulaphouca Poulaphouca
Poulaphouca Poulaphouca.

THE YEWS: *(Mingling their boughs)*
Listen. Whisper. She is right, our sister.
We grew by Poulaphouca waterfall. We
gave shade on languorous summer days.

JOHN WYSE NOLAN: *(In the background,
in Irish National Forester's uniform, doffs his
plumed hat)* Prosper! Give shade on languorous days, trees of Ireland!

THE YEWS: *(Murmuring)* Who came to
Poulaphouca with the high school ex-
cursion? Who left his nutquesting classmates to seek our shade?

BLOOM: *(Pigeonbreasted, bottleshouldered,
padded, in nondescript juvenile grey and black
striped suit, too small for him, white tennis
shoes, bordered stockings with turnover tops,
and a red school cap with badge)* I was in my
teens, a growing boy.

. . .

THE ECHO: Fool!

THE YEWS: *(Rustling)* She is right, our
sister. Whisper. *(Whispered kisses are heard
in all the wood. Faces of hamadryads peep out
from the boles and among the leaves and break
blossoming into bloom)* Who profaned our
silent shade?

THE NYMPH: *(Coyly through parting
fingers)* There! In the open air?

THE YEWS: *(Sweeping downward)* Sister,
yes. And on our virgin sward.

THE WATERFALL:
Poulaphouca Poulaphouca
Phoucaphouca Phoucaphouca.

THE NYMPH: *(With wide fingers)* O! In-
famy!

BLOOM: I was precocious. Youth. The
fauns. I sacrificed to the god of the
forest. The flowers that bloom in the
spring. It was pairing time.

Poulaphouca waterfall, Co. Kildare

*Ulysses*

But, as he confidently anticipated, there was not a sign of a Jehu plying for hire anywhere to be seen except a four-wheeler, probably engaged by some fellows inside on the spree, outside the North Star Hotel and there was no symptom of its budging a quarter of an inch when Mr Bloom, who was anything but a professional whistler, endeavoured to hail it by emitting a kind of a whistle, holding his arms arched over his head, twice.

This was a quandary but, bringing commonsense to bear on it, evidently there was nothing for it but put a good face on the matter and foot it which they accordingly did. So, bevelling around by Mullet's and the Signal House, which they shortly reached, they proceeded perforce in the direction of Amiens street railway terminus, Mr Bloom being handicapped by the circumstance that one of the back buttons of his trousers had, to vary the time-honoured adage, gone the way of all buttons, though, entering thoroughly into the spirit of the thing, he heroically made light of the mischance.

*Above:* the North Star Hotel in Amiens Street
*Right:* Amiens Street Station, now Connolly Station

126

*Ulysses*

– Murphy's my name, the sailor continued, W. B. Murphy, of Carrigaloe. Know where that is?

– Queenstown Harbour, Stephen replied.

– That's right, the sailor said. Fort Camden and Fort Carlisle. That's where I hails from. My little woman's down there. She's waiting for me, I know. *For England, home and beauty*. She's my own true wife I haven't seen for seven years now, sailing about.

Mr Bloom could easily picture his advent on this scene – the homecoming to the mariner's roadside shieling after having diddled Davy Jones – a rainy night with a blind moon. Across the world for a wife. Quite a number of stories there were on that particular Alice Ben Bolt topic, Enoch Arden and Rip van Winkle and does anybody hereabouts remember Caoc O'Leary, a favourite and most trying declamation piece, by the way, of poor John Casey and a bit of perfect poetry in its own small way?

The harbour at Cobh, formerly known as Queenstown, Co. Cork

*Ulysses*

*Ulysses*

What action did Bloom make on their arrival at their destination?

At the housesteps of the 4th of the equidifferent uneven numbers, number 7 Eccles street, he inserted his hand mechanically into the back pocket of his trousers to obtain his latchkey.

Was it there?

It was in the corresponding pocket of the trousers which he had worn on the day but one preceding.

Why was he doubly irritated?

Because he had forgotten and because he remembered that he had reminded himself twice not to forget.

What were then the alternatives before the, premeditatedly (respectively) and inadvertently, keyless couple?

To enter or not to enter. To knock or not to knock.

Bloom's decision?

A stratagem. Resting his feet on the dwarf wall, he climbed over the area railings, compressed his hat on his head, grasped two points at the lower union of rails and stiles, lowered his body gradually by its length of five feet nine inches and a half to within two feet ten inches of the area pavement, and allowed his body to move freely in space by separating himself from the railings and crouching in preparation for the impact of the fall.

Did he fall?

By his body's known weight of eleven stone and four pounds in avoirdupois measure, as certified by the graduated machine for periodical selfweighing in the premises of Francis Frœdman, pharmaceutical chemist of 19 Frederick street, north. . . .

*Above:* the 'Holy Door' is enshrined in the Bailey Bar and Restaurant in Duke Street

*Left:* no. 78 Eccles Street is identical to Bloom's home at no.7, which no longer exists

The Glencree dinner. Alderman Robert O'Reilly emptying the port into his soup before the flag fell, Bobbob lapping it for the inner alderman. Couldn't hear what the band played. For what we have already received may the Lord make us. Milly was a kiddy then. Molly had that elephantgrey dress with the braided frogs. Mantailored with selfcovered buttons . . . . Never put a dress on her back like it. Fitted her like a glove, shoulder and hips. Just beginning to plump it out well. Rabbit pie we had that day. People looking after her.

– There was a big spread out at Glencree reformatory, Lenehan said eagerly. The annual dinner you know. Boiled shirt affair. The lord mayor was there, Val Dillon it was . . . .

Lenehan linked his arm warmly.

– But wait till I tell you, he said. We had a midnight lunch too after all the jollification and when we sallied forth it was blue o'clock the morning after the night before. Coming home it was a gorgeous winter's night on the Featherbed Mountain. Bloom and Chris Callinan were on one side of the car and I was with the wife on the other. We started singing glees and duets: *Lo, the early beam of morning*. She was well primed with a good load of Delahunt's port under her bellyband. Every jolt the bloody car gave I had her bumping up against me. Hell's delights! She has a fine pair, God bless her. Like that.

'Parallax' at work: Bloom's view of the Glencree evening, followed by Lenehan's account, followed *overleaf* by Molly's
*Right:* the Glencree Reformatory, now a peace centre known as St Kevin's

*Ulysses*

Lenehans ... that sponger he was making free with me after the Glencree dinner coming back that long joult over the featherbed mountain after the lord Mayor looking at me with his dirty eyes Val Dillon that big heathen

*Ulysses*

Glowing wine on his palate lingered swallowed. Crushing in the winepress grapes of Burgundy. Sun's heat it is. Seems to a secret touch telling me memory. Touched his sense moistened remembered. Hidden under wild ferns on Howth. Below us bay sleeping sky. No sound. The sky. The bay purple by the Lion's head. Green by Drumleck. Yellowgreen towards Sutton. Fields of undersea, the lines faint brown in grass, buried cities. Pillowed on my coat she had her hair, earwigs in the heather scrub my hand under her nape, you'll toss me all. O wonder! Coolsoft with ointments her hand touched me, caressed: her eyes upon me did not turn away. Ravished over her I lay, full lips full open, kissed her mouth . . . . Flowers her eyes were, take me, willing eyes. Pebbles fell. She lay still. A goat. No-one. High on Ben Howth rhododendrons a nannygoat walking surefooted, dropping currants. Screened under ferns she laughed warmfolded. Wildly I lay on her, kissed her; eyes, her lips, her stretched neck, beating, woman's breasts full in her blouse of nun's veiling, fat nipples upright. Hot I tongued her. She kissed me. I was kissed. All yielding she tossed my hair. Kissed, she kissed me.

Me. And me now.

All quiet on Howth now. The distant hills seem. Where we. The rhododendrons. I am a fool perhaps. He gets the plums and I the plumstones. Where I come in. All that old hill has seen.

the sun shines for you he said the day we were lying among the rhododendrons on Howth head in the grey tweed suit and his straw hat the day I got him to propose to me yes first I gave him the bit of seedcake out of my mouth and it was leapyear like now yes 16 years ago my God after that long kiss I near lost my breath yes he said I was a flower of the mountain yes so we are flowers all a womans body yes that was one true thing he said in his life and the sun shines for you today yes that was why I liked him because I saw he understood or felt what a woman is and I knew I could always get round him and I gave him all the pleasure I could leading him on till he asked me to say yes and I wouldnt answer first only looked out over the sea and the sky

Bloom and Molly remembering rhododendrons on the Hill of Howth

# FINNEGANS WAKE

The great fall of the offwall entailed at such short notice the pftjschute of Finnegan, erse solid man, that the humpty-hillhead of humself prumptly sends an unquiring one well to the west in quest of his tumptytumtoes:

Finnegan, or Humphrey, has become the 'humptyhillhead' of Howth

riverrun, past Eve and Adam's, from swerve of shore to bend of bay, brings us by a commodius vicus of recirculation back to Howth Castle and Environs.

St Francis of Assisi – whose Dublin nickname is 'Adam and Eve's' – on Merchant's Quay

*Finnegans Wake*

And the all gianed in with the shout-most shoviality. Agog and magog and the round of them agrog. To the continuation of that celebration until Hanandhunigan's extermination! Some in kinkin corass, more, kankan keening. Belling him up and filling him down. He's stiff but he's steady is Priam Olim! 'Twas he was the dacent gaylabouring youth. Sharpen his pillowsconc, tap up his bier! E'erawhere in this whorl would ye hear sich a din again? With their deepbrow fundigs and the dusty fidelios. They laid him brawdawn alanglast bed. With a bockalips of finisky fore his feet. And a barrowload of guenesis hoer his head. Tee the tootal of the fluid hang the twoddle of the fuddled, O!

'Phil the Fluter's Ball' mingles with 'Brian O'Lynn', 'Finnegan's Wake' and other Dublin street songs

safe in bed as he dreamed that he'd wealthes in mormon halls when wokenp by a fourth loud snore out of his land of byelo while hickstrey's maws was grazing in the moonlight by hearing hammering on the pandywhank scale emanating from the blind pig and anything like it (oonagh! oonagh!) in the whole history of the Mullingcan Inn he never. This battering babel allower the door and sideposts, he always said, was not in the very remotest like the belzey babble of a bottle of boose which would not rouse him out o' slumber deep but reminded him loads more of the martiallawsey marses of foreign musikants' instrumongs or the overthrewer to the third last days of Pompery . . . .

[HCE] is a prince of the fingallian in a hiberniad of hoolies; has a hodge to wherry him and a frenchy to curry him and a brabanson for his beeter and a fritz at his switch; was waylaid of a parker and beschotten by a buckeley; kicks lintils when he's cuppy and casts Jacob's arroroots, dime after dime, to poor waifstrays on the perish; reads the charms of H. C. Endersen all the weaks of his evenin and the crimes of Ivaun the Taurrible every strongday morn; soaps you soft to your face and slaps himself when he's badend; owns the bulgiest bungbarrel that ever was tiptapped in the privace of the Mullingar Inn;

Mullingar House in Chapelizod where *Finnegans Wake* is dreamed

Hence when the clouds roll by, jamey, a proudseye view is enjoyable of our mounding's mass, now Wallinstone national museum, with, in some greenish distance, the charmful waterloose country and the two quitewhite villagettes who hear show of themselves so gigglesomes minxt the follyages, the prettilees! Penetrators are permitted into the museomound free. Welsh and the Paddy Patkinses, one shelenk!

The Wellington ('Wallinstone') Monument in Phoenix Park

*Finnegans Wake*

145

*Finnegans Wake*

It was ages behind that when nullahs were nowhere, in county Wickenlow, garden of Erin, before she ever dreamt she'd lave Kilbride and go foaming under Horsepass bridge, with the great southerwestern windstorming her traces and the midland's grainwaster asarch for her track, to wend her ways byandby, robecca or worse, to spin and to grind, to swab and to thrash, for all her golden lifey in the barleyfields and pennylotts of Humphrey's fordofhurdlestown . . . .

Horsepass Bridge, Co. Wicklow

She was just a young thin pale soft shy slim slip of a thing then, sauntering, by silvamoonlake and he was a heavy trudging lurching lieabroad of a Curraghman, making his hay for whose sun to shine on, as tough as the oaktrees (peats be with them!) used to rustle that time down by the dykes of killing Kildare, for forstfellfoss with a plash across her.

*Overleaf:*
Kevin, having been graunted the praviloge of a priest's postcreated portable *altare cum balneo,* when espousing the one true cross, invented and exalted, in celibate matrimony at matin chime arose and westfrom went and came in alb of cloth of gold to our own midmost Glendalough-le-vert by archangelical guidance where amiddle of meeting waters of river Yssia and Essia river on this one of eithers lone navigable lake

*Finnegans Wake*

Before there was patch at all on Ireland there lived a lord at Lucan. We only wish everyone was as sure of anything in this watery world as we are of everything in the newlywet fellow that's bound to follow.

Castletown House, near Lucan, Co. Kildare

*Finnegans Wake*

154

an enysled lakelet yslanding a lacustrine yslet, whercupon with beached raft sub-diaconal bath *propter* altar, with oil extremely anointed, accompanied by prayer, holy Kevin bided till the third morn hour but to build a rubric penitential honeybeehivehut in whose enclosure to live in fortitude, acolyte of cardinal virtues,

St Kevin's beehive hut where Kevin the hermit-saint tried to isolate himself from the temptation of beautiful young Cathleen

Can't hear with the waters of. The chittering waters of. Flittering bats, field-mice bawk talk. Ho! Are you not gone ahome? What Thom Malone? Can't hear with bawk of bats, all thim liffeying waters of. Ho, talk save us! My foos won't moos. I feel as old as yonder elm. A tale told of Shaun or Shem? All Livia's daughter-sons. Dark hawks hear us. Night! Night! My ho head halls. I feel as heavy as yonder stone. Tell me of John or Shaun? Who were Shem and Shaun the living sons or daughters of? Night now! Tell me, tell me, tell me, elm! Night night! Telmetale of stem or stone. Beside the rivering waters of, hitherandthithering waters of. Night!

Anna Liffey flows into the night

sad and weary I go back to you, my cold father, my cold mad father, my cold mad feary father, till the near sight of the mere size of him, the moyles and moyles of it, moananoaning, makes me seasilt saltsick and I rush, my only, into your arms. I see them rising! Save me from those therrble prongs! Two more. Onetwo moremens more. So. Avelaval. My leaves have drifted from me. All. But one clings still. I'll bear it on me. To remind me of. Lff! So soft this morning, ours. Yes. Carry me along, taddy, like you done through the toy fair! If I seen him bearing down on me now under whitespread wings like he'd come from Arkangels, I sink I'd die down over his feet, humbly dumbly, only to washup. Yes, tid. There's where. First. We pass through grass behush the bush to. Whish! A gull. Gulls. Far calls. Coming, far! End here. Us then. Finn, again! Take. Bussoftlhee, mememormee! Till thousendsthee. Lps. The keys to. Given! A way a lone a last a loved a long the

*Finnegans Wake*

# READING ABOUT JOYCE

Books on Joyce are legion. Three good short studies are, Harry Levin's *James Joyce: A Critical Introduction*, as good as ever after fifty years; Anthony Burgess's *Here Comes Everybody*, for a quirky, entertaining study by a novelist who knows Joyce from the inside, and John Gross's *Joyce*, a model of compressed commonsense and imaginative sympathy. One longer, more academic study, C. H. Peake's *James Joyce: the Citizen and the Artist*, to be read with some judicious skipping, offers the student a clear, organized, unpretentious account of what's going on in Joyce's major works.

For Joyce's life, try two books by men who knew him well: the painter Frank Budgen's genial but shrewd account of Joyce in his *Ulysses* days, *James Joyce and the Making of Ulysses*, and *My Brother's Keeper*, an equally shrewd but considerably more exasperated account by Stanislaus Joyce of his dealings with an ever-importunate brother. Richard Ellmann's enormous, admirably painstaking *James Joyce* (revised edition, 1982) links the life and the work most fruitfully, and Brenda Maddox's recent *Nora* adds a valuable new angle on the whole Joycean enterprise.